THE
BAG LADY
PAPERS

ALSO BY
ALEXANDRA PENNEY
....

How to Make Love to a Man
How to Make Love to Each Other

THE
BAG LADY
PAPERS

The Priceless Experience of Losing It All

ALEXANDRA PENNEY

voice

HYPERION   NEW YORK

Library of Congress Cataloging-in-Publication Data

Penney, Alexandra.
  The bag lady papers: the priceless experience of losing it all / Alexandra Penney.
    p. cm.
  ISBN 978-1-4013-4118-3
  1. Penney, Alexandra. 2. Penney, Alexandra—Finance, Personal. 3. Madoff, Bernard L. 4. Swindlers and swindling—United States—Case studies. 5. Investments—United States—Case studies. 6. Financial security—United States—Case studies. 7. Women periodical editors—United States—Biography. 8. Periodical editors—United States—Biography. 9. Women authors, American—Biography. 10. New York (N.Y.)—Biography. I. Title.
  CT275.P5556A3 2009
    364.16'3092—dc22
    [B]   2009037379

Hyperion books are available for special promotions and premiums. For details contact the HarperCollins Special Markets Department in the New York office at 212-207-7528, fax 212-207-7222, or email spsales@harpercollins.com.

Book design by Shubhani Sarkar

FIRST EDITION

10   9   8   7   6   5   4   3

THIS LABEL APPLIES TO TEXT STOCK

We try to produce the most beautiful books possible, and we are also extremely concerned about the impact of our manufacturing process on the forests of the world and the environment as a whole. Accordingly, we've made sure that all of the paper we use has been certified as coming from forests that are managed to ensure the protection of the people and wildlife dependent upon them.

FOR JOHN
FOR ERIN
FOR DENNIS

CONTENTS

·······································

CONTENTS

Some of the names in this book have been changed to protect the privacy of friends and family.

GLOSSARY

....

MF   Bernard Madoff, aka MotherFucker

BMF   Before MF, life before Madoff

AMF   After MF, life after Madoff

MLS   Major Life Savers, friends who helped big-time

AAA   Activity Alleviates Anxiety, a tactic to ease panic
            attacks

PJ   Private Jet

PoRC   Person[s] of Reduced Circumstances

SNT   Stop Negative Thinking!

NSP   No Self Pity!

WoCA   Woman of a Certain Age

THE
BAG LADY
PAPERS

Introduction

For many years, I've feared that one day I'll wake up and be destitute and alone. I won't have enough money to feed myself or to pay the medical bills. I will have to hole up in a rusted-out car or in a closet-size room with peeling green paint and a single lightbulb swaying from a frayed greasy cord, or I will end up trudging the streets, cold and abandoned, with a shopping cart filled with tattered bags full of god knows what.

If you Google "bag lady fears" or "bag lady syndrome" you will quickly learn that it isn't in the *DSM*, the psychiatrist's bedside reference book, but that it has affected Lily Tomlin, Gloria Steinem, Shirley MacLaine, and many other accomplished, well-known women, who all admit to being haunted by the fear of becoming a bag lady. In the past months

I have talked with dozens of women of all ages and backgrounds who have revealed their own dark bag lady visions. The fear cuts across social and economic groups, and it is felt mostly by women. You can be making millions of bucks and still harbor scary images of yourself as a bag lady.

In December 2008, my worst nightmare came true. I found out I was dead broke. I had lost all my savings in the colossal Ponzi scheme of Bernard Madoff, forthwith to be known as the MF, which in plain English stands for "motherfucker," the worst name I can think of.

I am a visual artist and have no aspirations to be a full-time writer or a memoirist. For several years I was a journalist reporting other people's stories. Writing in the revelatory first person is an uneasy task for me, but I decided to tell about what happened to me by writing a blog. I needed to earn money immediately and the blog, although it paid very little, was a start. I wrote that I had worked hard from the time I was sixteen and made good wages for that work. I married, divorced, and raised a precious son on my own.

I admitted that I love luxurious things. I admitted to owning forty white shirts (they add up when you keep them from college days). I confessed that I had a housekeeper who came three mornings a week; elegant china; a 1995 dented Mercedes station wagon; a white, tenth-hand, twenty-year-old Chrysler LeBaron convertible that cost less than a Chanel jacket and is too dangerous and broken down to drive (thanks, GM).

I was both frustrated and heartened by readers' reactions; frustrated because many people felt I was a privileged, greedy, and uncaring elitist who deserved to lose my money. And heartened because many people voiced their own fears and anxieties in response to my story.

It is curious that the bloggers who responded seemed obsessed with a few particular details. There was a huge guessing game about how old I am. According to the bloggers I'm somewhere between forty-five and eighty-nine. I left out my age purposely. Ever since I was a beauty editor at *Glamour* magazine and saw firsthand that the surface facts of chronological age are meaningless, I've believed that you are what age you think you are. Right now I'm starting all over and I would guess my age to be pretty damn young. But why does it matter so intensely? No matter how old you are, serious loss is a catastrophic experience.

The bloggers also want to know exactly how much money I entrusted to Madoff. Why? Why do they care so much? What does it mean? Well, I can't give exact amounts for legal reasons, but my point is that I lost everything I worked for over many years.

I am not writing this book to whine or to complain, but in the first couple of months I was so panicked that I found myself constantly groaning about what had happened. It may sound tiresome now but that was the unvarnished reality of the way I felt. I am always deeply aware that others confront far more dire situations than mine. As I heard from many men and women from across America, Europe, and even Asia, who wrote me with their own stories, I felt that it might be helpful to tell about what it is like to have your worst fears realized and how it is possible to get on with your life when it seems in total ruin.

I believe the landslide of responses to my blog also signaled that something enormous is going on here and now in America—a reckoning and recalibrating of money, class, status, and society. We've all had to make adjustments and transitions. Estimates suggest that the 2009 economic meltdown will last for as long as five years, perhaps even longer. We are living in a new world that is careening in unknown directions at an undreamed of speed.

Change is scary and daunting and exciting at the same time. It has the power to paralyze or galvanize. Change unnerves. Disorients. Distorts. In one minute my life and my hopes for the future changed completely. I could cower under my covers for god knows how long, or I could face the fears and challenges of my new situation and survive with humanity and grace and humor.

When you experience loss or change you will surprise yourself. I am definitely getting through; I am moving on—and up. I'm welcoming new experiences, I'm off on new adventures, I'm finding out what's important and what's not worth a second glance. Most of all, I have surprised myself by actually having a great time even in the few months right after the debacle. I lost it all, but I am coming out on top, and I now realize that in many ways this is because of the life I've led and the significant lessons I've learned along the way.

CHAPTER 1

December 11, 2008

I am carefully placing Baccarat crystal goblets on my dining room table. The lacquered pear-wood is set for four, with starched white place mats and napkins, pretty flowered English antique plates, and a handful of white votive candles. Five small silver vases filled with white freesia and the first delicate white tulips that signal spring will be on the way—and the sooner the better. Even though it is just mid-December, it seems as if it's been forever winter here in steely gray New York, with four snowfalls and single-digit windchill factors that invade the bones and frost the soul.

I have lived in this sun-filled apartment with wide views of the East River for almost twenty years, and I love to entertain here. Good friends will arrive soon and I have dug up my ancient Julia Child cookbook to make dessert. It's so old the covers have fallen off, but the Grand Marnier soufflé is a wow and actually very easy to prepare. In the kitchen the soufflé is waiting in its mold so I can pop it into the oven as soon as everyone is here.

The phone rings and I answer it.

"I'm hoping it's a rumor," a very dear friend, Alex, says, "but Bernard Madoff's just been arrested. All your money's with him, right?"

Jesus Christ!!!! All!! Every cent I ever saved since I started working summers at Lord & Taylor when I was sixteen years old. *This cannot be true!*

My cell phone begins to ring. The screen shows that it's my son calling from California. I hang up with Alex and my son repeats the news: "Don't worry, Mom, everything will be okay. We love you and you can always stay in our guest house."

I am grateful to the point of tears for the offer. But I am not going to be a burden to anyone. I never have been and I never will be.

I call Paul, my closest friend and on-and-off longtime companion, who's on his way to my place for dinner, and tell him what's happened.

"Please take a taxi and get here as fast as you humanly can. I can't be alone. I'm beyond physically terrified. And would you call Will and Jae and tell them not to come over? They'll understand."

I phone my lawyer and leave a message that I've lost all my money with Bernard Madoff and that I need to see him ASAP.

Whenever anxiety avalanches over me, I am compelled

to clean whatever is in sight, to collect things and put them into tidy piles. This is one of those moments.

The soufflé has fallen in its mold. How fitting! My world is collapsing as well. I take the silver, linens, and candles off the table and place them precisely back in their drawers and cabinets.

I pause at the flowers. I bought them late this afternoon, as I usually do before a dinner party. Will I ever be able to afford fresh flowers again? Since college days, when I hung out in the musky, humid botany conservatory to escape the freezing New England cold, I have loved flowers. To see a magnificent rose unfurl its petals and reveal its fragrance freely to the world, and then to give itself quietly back to nature, has always been a wonder to me. So, instead of tossing the freesia and tulips, I take them out of the silver vases and place them carefully in a couple of drinking glasses and add some water. The little vases go into their corner cupboard, the remains of the soufflé are emptied into the garbage, and the soufflé mold is scoured.

Oh god, there's the meat loaf still cooking in the oven. I scoop it out of the pan, and even though it's too hot, I wrap it in foil with neat corners and put it in the refrigerator alongside the caramelized walnut and arugula salad I've made for an appetizer. I scrub that pan, too, wash it, dry it, and store it under the counter alongside the other organized rows of pots and cookware.

The last thing on the table is the crystal. I carry each heavy goblet to the glass-fronted cabinet where their lovely facets catch the light. I bought the Baccarat piece by piece because, twenty-five years ago, I didn't have the money to buy more than one glass at a time. As I'm putting the last one away, Paul flies in the door and gives me a huge hug, which has the unintended effect of physically reassuring me that I am not in some sort of weird dream state. He's canceled the other two dinner guests.

I stand in my spotless kitchen and haven't the faintest idea of what to do. He gives me another hug, then clicks on the television and the computer. He's scanning the channels and Googling Madoff. Apparently, the MF confessed to his sons and to the FBI that he has put all his investors into a giant Ponzi scheme. Nothing much else is clear, but I have a gut certainty that I have lost it all.

Terror snakes through my veins. The phone rings again. I'm still standing, dumbstruck, in the kitchen. It's another friend, Gayle, who says, "I had money in Madoff, too. What are you going to do?"

I don't know what to tell her. She doesn't know what to tell me. All we can do is agree to stay in close touch and hang up.

The call, at least, has broken the spell that seemed to have cemented my feet to my black-and-white-tiled kitchen floor. I make my way to my desk in the library and take out all the MF's statements, which have appeared so real and reassuring to me over the past years. There were the stocks he'd bought: Apple, Google, Hewlett-Packard, Exxon-Mobil, Bank of America, and many others, all familiar names to me. I look more closely. On the bottom line I see that he had put all my money into United States Treasury bills at the end of October.

In my panic, I'd forgotten about the Treasury bills. A few weeks ago, in the beginning of November, I had not received the MF's usual financial paperwork, which unfailingly arrived in the first week of the month. I had wondered why. I wanted to redeem my retirement money and have it in cash, out of the fund. The market was going crazy and I was at least smart enough to know it was no time to be in any kind of stock market investment, legendary or not.

I had waited a couple of days more for the statement to arrive, just to make sure there wasn't a post office delay, then I phoned Madoff headquarters on November 11; I remember the day because it was my father's birthday. Over the ten years that my savings were with the MF, I had called the office only two or three times about some procedural matter, in each instance speaking to a different person who appeared knowledgeable when I gave my name and account number.

The woman who took my call on November 11 told me that the statements were to be mailed out "tomorrow" and that someone would get back to me about redeeming my money.

"You have no worries," she said that day, "you're in United States Treasuries."

I called again a few days later and was informed that the statements "had gone out" and, once more, all was well, I was in Treasury bills, which were "one hundred percent safe." Still, I replied that I wanted to take my money out of my account. Someone would get back to me as soon as possible, she said.

I was momentarily lulled because the last paperwork had been issued a few short weeks ago, in October, and because the woman at Bernard L. Madoff Investment Securities had repeatedly reassured me that I was in United States Treasury bills.

As I now check the computerized pages of the October statement, I feel a tendril of hope. My money is backed by the American government! Maybe I haven't lost it all.

I call Gayle back excitedly, and we compare statements. She has Treasuries, too. But when we examine the paperwork closely, we realize that the numbers of the bills are exactly the same. Motherfucker! These are fake, too.

Gayle and I hang up again and I start pounding the computer keys to find the number of the United States Department of the Treasury in Washington, D.C. I locate the number, dial, and a machine asks me to leave a voice message.

I say my name and explain, "I am a client of Bernard Madoff. I understand he's been arrested for fraud and I would like to check on a Treasury bill number. If someone could please call me back, I would be most appreciative."

I know it is ridiculous to phone the United States Treasury at this hour. But what else can I do? The apartment is spotlessly clean. I need activity to help alleviate my anxiety. Suddenly I remember that I have stashed away one very strong tranquilizer in the bathroom medicine chest in case there should be a death in the family. Well, there it is. My money has passed away. I pop the pill in my mouth.

Alex's husband, Byron, rings up to remind me of Emerson's line, "I am defeated all the time, but I am born to victory."

I am thanking him when the other line rings. "This is Mr. W, from the United States Department of the Treasury," a deep voice says.

It's past eight at night, and the U.S. Treasury is returning my call? I am now even more horribly certain that this Madoff thing is real and that I am standing in the middle of a nightmare.

I tell him that I have a Treasury bill and want to check the number to see if it is real.

"I've heard from about fifteen Madoff clients," he says before asking me the bill number.

"That is indeed a Treasury offering. And there are many entities that would buy that offering."

"How can I find out if Madoff is one of them?" I ask.

"I don't think there is any place where you can find out who bought what," he responds.

"There must be a way," I plead. "Do you have any idea how I could go about it?"

"It sounds like a bad situation and I am sorry but I can't offer advice," he says with finality.

The tranquilizer is hitting me like a tsunami. Paul tells me he'll spend the night, since he doesn't think I should be alone. I'm so groggy that I don't know how to tell him how grateful I am, so I give him one last hug and head for bed. He stays glued to the TV, scanning the channels for more news and details on the situation. All the cable stations are covering the story.

I don't turn out the lights. I start up the laptop that's on my night table. A thought has been hovering in my mind since Alex and my son called, and it's a thought that many before me have had upon receiving devastating news. It's the universal out, the final option, that, like it or not, exists for everyone. I Google the Hemlock Society. I want to know a painless way to die. The Hemlock Society Web site, it turns out, has been dismantled; it has gone to cyber heaven. If I weren't in such a morbid state, I'd have a good laugh about that.

I check out a few more sites that pop up after I search for "self-inflicted death." I learn that, unfortunately, it takes a while to cross the Styx to get to the otherworld, such as it may be. If you're in a major hurry, guns work fast, as does jumping out of windows, and cyanide, which is used in making jewelry, seems to work best and is speediest. I love jewelry, especially pearls, so this link to the chemical that could end it all seems to reflect perfectly the irony and absurdity of what is happening to me. Before I can find out more, the tranquilizer takes over and, mercifully, I pass out.

CHAPTER 2

AAA—Activity Alleviates Anxiety

Something terrible has happened but I can't remember what it is. I stumble out of bed, turn on the TV, step into the shower, and stay there for almost half an hour with hot water streaming over me, hoping the negative ions will help lessen the head-to-toe panic.

I am paralyzed by the early-morning news bulletins. More terrifying thoughts assault me, horrid visions of state-run institutions for sick old people where sloe-eyed attendants drug you and strap you to wheelchairs.

Paul has left a note on my mirror saying that he had to leave for his studio and to call him right away if I need anything. He'll check in with me later. I open the front door and *The New York Times,* as usual, is right there. I can bear only to glance at the headlines. It's all there: the MF's confession, the Ponzi scheme, his admission that everything was a lie.

I'm close to nauseous with anxiety, but, once again, I must do something. I can't sit here alone. Then an idea hits me: I will go to the MF's offices. They are just two blocks away.

I dress as I would for any other day of working in the studio—jeans, freshly ironed white shirt, Hermès Kelly bag (purchased when I was an editor at Condé Nast—how much can I get for it on eBay, I wonder?), goosedown jacket with a fur collar, and small gold earrings from my mother. Dressing carefully in my normal clothes puts a bit of consoling distance between me and my bag lady fears.

It's not even eight a.m. when I get to Madoff's building, but already people are milling around in the lobby. I am not the only one who has dressed for the occasion—fur coats abound. One older woman who is perfectly groomed and swathed in golden sable is leaning on the arm of her husband, whose face is the color of green-gray bread mold.

I approach the lobby guard and say, "We are Madoff clients and we need to go up to his office please." Part of me knows this will never happen, but part of me thinks that as of yesterday, anything can happen.

When people hear me politely but firmly asking to be let upstairs, they all chime in. The blond woman in sable says to me, "You've got the right attitude. Let's get up there! I've lost everything, everything."

I wonder how much "everything" means. Does she still have a huge Park Avenue apartment, a silvery Maybach, a villa in Tuscany?

I don't, but I'm certainly a lot better off than many of these victims. I have a modest one-bedroom getaway house on Long Island that I bought ten years ago. I thought owning real estate would always be a good investment. I had a mortgage on the house and recently took out a home equity loan on it as well, after listening to the advice of two different financial and tax planners who had been highly recommended by smart friends. Madoff was generating a steady ten percent return and the loans on the house were around six percent, so, as the planners explained, the four-percent margin was meaningful.

I kept upping the home equity loan and taking out money from it to pay for living and my photography studio expenses rather than depleting my Madoff money so that my savings with him would continue to grow. This morning I know that the Long Island shack, as I call it, will have to be sold ASAP. I have no money to cover the loan costs. Or even the gas and electricity bills. I've been living off the proceeds from my photographs and small withdrawals from my Madoff account every quarter since I started renting my photography studio two years ago.

I also bought an inexpensive one-bedroom bungalow in Florida a couple of years ago with some of the money I'd made from writing and several of my photographs. The Florida place was part of a pension plan that was set up by an accountant years ago when I first started to save money. I couldn't live or vacation in the Florida house because of my pension plan's legal restrictions, but I always hoped it would be a good investment. I painted the floors, walls, ceilings, and everything in sight in white, found some stylish white furniture at Ikea so that it would be an attractive place and I could rent it out to cover its costs. Now I'll have to sell it, too. Whatever I can make on it won't even come close to covering half the loans I owe for the house on Long Island—that is, if I can make anything at all. Home values in Florida have plummeted to the worst lows in the nation. And from what I've read it doesn't look as if this will change anytime soon, but I have no time to wait for a real estate upswing.

And of course there's my apartment. I am hoping that if I can sell the rest I can stay in this place where I have lived for so long. If I can just remain in my home I will have some peace of mind, even if I have no more than a pittance to live on. Staying in my home would help me to get my bearings again and give me some sense of continuity. But who knows if anything will sell—or when? Every single aspect of my life is uncertain at this moment. Not knowing is hell. The worst kind of emotional hell.

Right now, standing in the expanding crowd in the MF's lobby, I will myself not to think about the apartment or I will have some sort of epic panic attack.

The group is young, old, in between. Some people look like bicycle messengers, others could be pharmacists and librarians, and a good percentage look as if they go to the right barbers and have had subtle but expensive Botox jobs and minilifts.

Finally, a man descends from the upper reaches of the MF's establishment. He informs us that he is a lawyer and his name is Lee Richards. He is the interim "receiver" for bankruptcy proceedings. He states coolly that it will take days or even months to establish any real facts. The crowd asks: "Is there any money there?" "Can we get insurance?"

One woman says, "I have only a small bank account left. I can't live on it. What should I do?" Of course Lee Richards doesn't answer. He tells us there is to be some sort of motion in federal court downtown this afternoon; Bernard Madoff will make an appearance before the judge.

....

I had called my internist's office the minute it was open for business this morning. Now, after being sent away from the MF's lobby, I race to pick up my prescription for tranquilizers. At the Madison Avenue pharmacy where I've had a charge account since my son was a baby, I wait a few minutes for my prescription, and while I wait, by habit, I check out the newest Chanel shades. From now on, I think grimly, I won't be able to afford even generic lipsticks at Duane Reade. When I was the beauty editor at *Glamour* magazine for a couple of years after college, I became infatuated with the expensive brands that messengers dropped off at our offices by the bagful, even though I quickly learned it was mostly chic packaging and seductive advertising that made them so costly and so "luxurious." To this day, buying a new lipstick at a department store has been a good pick-me-up when the world seems slightly out of whack.

Now, obviously, I need something more potent.

Twenty minutes after leaving the drugstore, I'm staring at portraits of stern, WASPy, white-shoe founding partners on the paneled walls of my attorney's reception area. My father was a lawyer, and I've always thought of most lawyers as boring or on the make for new clients. But who can resist Michael? He does uncanny Goofy imitations while reviewing a will or advising on tax matters. There's no laughing Michael today, though; instead, he is poring carefully over the MF's papers.

"It doesn't look good," he concludes. "These numbers don't match up." He says he'll talk to his colleagues who deal with securities fraud. There is an organization called Securities Investor Protection Corporation (SIPC) that maintains a special reserve insurance fund authorized by Congress to help investors at failed brokerage firms.

"Am I eligible for the SIPC fund?" I ask, for a moment allowing myself a smidgen of hope.

"There's no way of telling yet," he says. I reach into my bag for a tranquilizer.

My mind is flooding with panic again as I race-walk back home to pick up my BlackBerry, which I forgot in my rush to get out of the house. I need to be connected to my lawyer and to Paul and to my son and to my friends.

The phone is ringing as I walk in the door. It's Mr. W from the U.S. Treasury! I'm speechless. The U.S. Treasury has called me—twice in twenty-four hours!

Mr. W is polite and perhaps a bit sorrowful as he says, "I'm calling to say that I haven't been able to locate a Web site where you might find out who bought the bills from that offering." I'm astounded by the phone call, but it tells me absolutely nothing.

Before I leave for the courthouse, where I will spend the afternoon waiting, fruitlessly, for the MF to appear, I call Ed Victor, the literary agent. He's represented me before and he's a good friend. One thing I know for sure is that I need work. Work and activity keep me sane and will prevent me from wallowing in self-pity or fear. I haven't written professionally for more than a decade, but maybe Ed can come up with something for me to do. I think of all the jobs I've had over the years, all the money I made that has vaporized in just one day. Oh my god, how will I ever earn enough money now?

Since the recession began, the art market has plummeted. I won't make a cent selling my photographs. At least if I sit and type, I can hold back the panic. Panic? What word is worse than "panic"? "Hysteria." "Implosion." "Full-scale terror." "Body-crippling shock."

I explain what's happening to Ed and tell him that I need work, ask if he has any ideas. Four minutes later he phones back and says, "Call Tina Brown, she wants you to do a blog on her new Web site, The Daily Beast."

This may not be the answer to my problems but at least it's a start, and when in a crunch, I've always lived by my personal acronym of AAA: Activity Alleviates Anxiety. Of course I'll call Tina—instantly.

I'm traumatized by the events of the last eighteen hours and I don't have a plan, but a blog is a first step. I've never been too much of a planner, with one notable exception—my finances. I've always been relentlessly curious and, for the most part, I've followed paths that I thought would lead to unusual experiences and new adventures. I've strongly believed in carpe diem while keeping one eye on financial security. And I learned early on that the only person I could depend on to take care of me was me.

CHAPTER 3

There Is No Such Word as "No"

I grew up in one of the affluent suburbs of New York. My father, a Harvard graduate and son of a Greek immigrant, was legal counsel to a Fortune 500 corporation. My mother, a grande dame type, was an intellectual prone to depression. My childhood was comfortable though lonely. I was six when my mother had a severe nervous breakdown that landed her for almost a year in Payne Whitney, a New York psychiatric hospital. I stayed with my ancient Greek grandmother in Boston. Her attention was focused on my aunt, who lived with us and was suffering through the terminal stages of breast cancer, and who died in the room next to mine. When my mother returned, she bought me books and clothes but spent many of her days in bed behind closed doors.

College offered a respite from the oppressive, uptight years at home. I graduated as a philosophy major from Smith, knowing that my goals were fundamentally different from those of other girls in my class, who talked about the biggest rock and the richest husband, preferably one who lived in Greenwich or Grosse Pointe or on the Main Line, the sort of man who raced in the America's Cup and did something arcane with money on Wall Street. My mother had instilled in me the notion that writers and poets were exciting and led interesting lives. I'd always loved to draw and dreamed of becoming an artist. My happiest times during college were weekends when I would escape Smith and take the train to New York, where I hung out in Greenwich Village at the Waverly Hotel on Washington Square and visited museums and art galleries on Fifty-seventh Street.

My father, on the other hand, made it clear when I was very young that I would not be inheriting any money so I'd better learn how to make it on my own. He was a distant man, not often given to overt expressions of emotion, but his anger and despair were palpable when he recalled the financial damage done to his family during the Depression. Those conversations engraved on my impressionable brain the need

> to be highly disciplined,
> to work hard,
> to be laser-focused,
> to be independent,
> and to save money.

The minute I graduated I began to look for any kind of job in New York, so I could write and paint at night or on weekends. I met a smart, handsome man on a blind date, a talented industrial designer who had made jewelry as one of his projects in college. Rick was from Greenwich, Connecticut, and had grown up in a beautiful house with wide, very green lawns. His parents owned a racing sailboat but he seemed like a maverick, and that's what I was on the lookout for. He proposed, but I was adamant that I didn't want to settle down; first, I wanted to explore Europe.

I had found a job through a listing in *The New York Times* at the Simplicity Pattern Company writing copy for their catalogs and Rick had a position at a small industrial design firm. We lived in a minuscule but tidy fourth-floor walk-up in mid-Manhattan and saved every cent we could for our European trip. Within a year we had enough money to spend eight months abroad. We left everything familiar behind in New York, and headed to Europe, where we never knew what was coming next. Nevertheless, no bag lady fears intruded on those happy and adventurous times.

....

Married, back in New York, I found a job writing more fatuous copy, my husband landed a job at one of the best industrial design firms in the country, and our son was born, truly the most adorable baby who ever graced this planet, if you ask his parents. I kept rationalizing that I could quit commercial writing when I had enough savings of my own, and be Georgia O'Keeffe, but devising endless catalog copy for patterns soon began to make me feel pathetic, so I decided it was time to make a move. Because I'd seen articles by Joan Didion and other writers I admired in *Vogue* and *Harper's Bazaar,* I wrote query letters to both magazines. I signed them in hot pink lipstick with a lipstick exclamation point after my last sentence:

I would love to work for you!

Even though I wanted very much to be taken seriously, I had a feeling that unorthodox, albeit frivolous-looking, letter styling might grab some attention.

Sure enough, a couple days after I mailed the letters, I received a yellow-and-black Western Union telegram from Condé Nast Publications asking me to telephone the Personnel department.

A telegram!

My first of many Condé Nast lessons: urgency at all costs! And all costs be damned!

I landed a job as a promotion editor at *Vogue,* which involved writing copy and supervising shoots for some of the advertisers who bought pages in the magazine. My department was headed by the publisher. I was assigned to a small, spotless white cubicle with wall-to-wall graphite-gray carpet and a large window. I typed out my copy on a gray IBM electric machine set on a five-foot-long white-painted Parsons table. *Vogue* editors, I quickly learned, did not work at pedestrian desks.

Urgency! was the first lesson I learned at *Vogue*. The most important tutorial, however, involved my boss, Miss G, a tall, imperious woman with the kind of poreless skin that you see in ads, perfectly coiffed hair, and couture outfits that made the clothes in Lord & Taylor's Designer Dress Salon, where I had worked during summers while I was at college, look as if they were manufactured in outer Mongolia. She was the first and only woman I have ever seen with grass-green eyes.

Miss G went to Paris twice a year for "collections." Her clothes and luggage were messengered to the office and one of her three assistants always packed her hand-monogrammed Vuittons. On this particular night before she was to leave for Europe, the assistants had done something unheard of—they had mysteriously disappeared. Miss G demanded to know where they were. No one could explain the situation. We dreaded what might happen to them in the morning.

It was five thirty, the time I always left the office so I could be home in time to cook dinner for my son and husband.

Miss G marched into my cubicle, and my heart started pounding. Even though I had done nothing wrong, I was certain I was about to be fired because she never left her office. We peons were always summoned to her lair where she worked—if that is what she actually did—at a spotless white-lacquered Parsons table enhanced with two white ceramic pots containing flawless white orchids, plus a white phone and white pens filled with emerald ink that was a close match to her extraordinary eyes. On a white cube table close by was a crystal pitcher containing ice water that was refreshed every two hours, flanked by two faceted Baccarat goblets. The walls were covered in leopard-printed silk with matching draperies, a chaise, and slipper chairs.

"I'm leaving for Paris tomorrow," she intoned, peering down at me from her emerald green–rimmed reading glasses. Of course I knew she was going to Paris. Everyone in the department was flashed the second she was away from her desk.

"My bags need packing," she commanded and strode away.

"But Miss G," I began to protest, trying to catch up to her. She stopped dead in her tracks. No one ever said "but" to Miss G.

"I have to get home. My son's nanny leaves at six sharp and he'll be alone. I can't reach my husband, he's at a meeting with clients."

She looked at me as if I didn't exist.

"There's no such word as 'no,'" she pronounced with icy finality and proceeded down the hall in an urgent but somehow stately pace to her lair. No other human moved like Miss G.

I needed the job but my son needed me more. For just this one time, I knew I had to find a way to do what she asked so I could hold on to the job. I have blocked from my memory how I finagled someone to stay with him that night. I carefully packed Miss G's elegant Vuittons and learned one of the great lessons of my professional life. *There is no such word as "no."*

CHAPTER 4

Rich Bitch

MF + 24 HOURS

I haven't told Carmina that I must let her go. She comes in three mornings a week, whirlwinds around, and voilà! The Frette sheets are changed, the floors are polished to a dark gleam, and even my white shirts are ironed. Smart and wise, she's worked with me for eight years and is a trusted adviser on clothes and men and plastic surgery.

Carmina needs money (who doesn't?). She sends it to her family in Bolivia. In the years she's worked for me, she's become a beloved part of my family. How am I going to tell her that I have no money, that I can't afford to pay her? I told her on Friday a disastrous thing had happened to me, but I just don't have the guts to say anything about letting her go. I'll wait until Wednesday.

Every day I wear a classic clean white shirt to my studio.

I've hoarded them since college days, and carefully stitch up my favorites when they get frayed at the collar. A few have fancy designer labels but most are "100 percent pinpoint cotton" from Lands' End. White shirts look great on pretty much everyone, but for me they also perform a psychological task: I feel crisp and confident and ready for work when I head out the door.

My work for the past two years has been at my studio. I wanted to be a painter when I graduated from college, and since then my dream was to someday have a studio of my own. I hadn't summoned the courage to rent one until recently, because my hopes of becoming a full-time artist had been put to the side many times, as I took other jobs to make money to support myself and my son. Now that I finally have a small but beautiful sun-washed space—Room 803, "A P Studio"—I am heartbroken to have to give it up, but the art market is dead and if I can't sell work, I won't have money to pay my bills. I need cash.

....

Tina Brown, an urgency queen like many of the editors at Condé Nast, where she and I worked for many years, has set a deadline for my first blog: it is due in twenty-four hours.

I haven't "written" anything in a long time. And I am a wreck from no sleep, no money, and insanely attacking bag lady fears. My friends Richard and Alex, both journalists, offer to help. They coax me out of my apartment to have breakfast in Zé Café, a friendly little place on the corner of my block. We discuss what I might say about the MF for The Daily Beast, and before I can order a second latte Alex has paid the bill and is pulling on her coat and saying, "Let's go up to my place. We'll help you write!"

Richard is the brilliant editor of a major magazine. He gave me a big break with my first editorial photography assignment. I've known Alex since we were both editors at *Glamour*. She drips smarts and style—and kindness. I call her Saint Alex and sometimes Nurse Alex, as she tends to a flock of friends, making sure we are well and thriving.

Uptown at Alex's spacious apartment, she hands us pens and pads of paper and offers us tea, coffee, and M&M's. Byron, her husband, another award-winning magazine editor, joins the group.

"What's the title of your blog?" someone asks.

"Oh Lord, oh Lord! Never wrote a blog! Don't even read blogs!" I am moaning, with many fake grimaces, much to their amusement. "The last thing I wrote was at least a century ago and it was a sex book."

"Okay," Richard says, donning his editorial demeanor, "let's hear about what happened when you heard about Madoff."

I start to talk. They take notes. I mention my deepest fears of becoming a bag lady. I remember the time when I was six, holding my mother's hand, and I saw an old woman using her stuffed and tattered shopping bags to shield her face from the arctic air near our home. Her bare ankles were red-veined poles stuck into cracked black shoes with torn newspaper sticking out at the heels. Her layers of shredded sweaters were held together with safety pins. Even when I was a kid I somehow knew she didn't have a place to live, that she was frightened and alone.

I vividly recall the image and tell the group that I have always feared being abandoned and penniless and ending up on the streets.

One of us—we are so conjoined in our thinking that later I don't remember if it was one of the other three or me—says, "That's it, that's the blog—The Bag Lady—it will be about your worst fears."

"Bag Lady Chronicles," someone else calls out.

We finally settle on The Bag Lady Papers. It's a perfect title that says exactly how I feel and what I want to write about. Half an hour later, with notes in my clammy-with-anxiety hands and some idea of how to proceed, Richard and I hop into a taxi, and he drops me at home.

I'm dazed but energized; I write several hundred words and shoot them through cyberspace to Tina. A few hours later, one of her editors, the sympathetic and smart Jane Spencer, arrives at my apartment and we work deep into the night on the first installment of The Bag Lady Papers.

I am totally unprepared for what follows after the first blog hits The Beast. I read a few comments on the first day. Then I stop reading.

There are hundreds of vitriolic readers who think I'm a rich bitch and an uncaring elitist who was greedy and a fool to put all my money with the MF. They say I'm exploiting Carmina, that I am completely out of touch with the world, prancing around in my starched white shirts and haughty attitudes. A friend who is horrified by the rage and the cruelty tells me that a commenter—anonymous of course—has written that he wishes I would fall seriously ill. Someone else wishes I'd "be cornholed in a dark alley."

But hundreds of others, the same friend reports to me, write that they understand and know what it's like to be in my shoes (Manolos then, Keds now), and to have lost every hard-earned cent that I saved for retirement. Or, to be more precise, to have it stolen.

I consider responding directly to the bloggers. Of going mano a mano with a challenge: Here's my personal e-mail, write me without the cloak of anonymity that lets you say any damn thing you like. Tell me about your own life and your own fears. Call me on the phone. Meet me in a coffee shop. I'd like to know more about you.

Meeting the bloggers via e-mail, phone, or even face-to-face could be a valuable experience or a waste of energy. I must use the hours I have to figure out how to make money, how to stay afloat, how to stay sane and stable and decent in a world that is unkind and unfair most, but not all, of the time.

....

My pay for the blog adds up to what I used to spend treating a friend to lunch at the Four Seasons restaurant. But it's a mountain of money to me now. I've also written a long piece for *The Sunday Times* of London. They're wiring me the fee. It can't happen fast enough.

Every day I still go to the studio, trying not to think

about how soon I will have to give it up. I arrive around six in the morning. I make notes for another blog and then focus on my photography with fanatical concentration.

Normally I would leave the studio around six or seven to join Paul or other friends for dinner. But since the MF catastrophe, I stay until nine or ten at night. Nonstop work helps to keep the ever-circling demons at bay. And really, I don't know what else to do with myself.

I've e-mailed and called the agent of the building to see if it would be possible to renegotiate my studio lease now that the real estate market is lurching downward with no bottom in sight. I mentioned bartering some art, but he hasn't called me back yet.

I don't think about eating while I'm working, so when I finally get home, I've been subsisting on what's around, some Progresso soup, nonfat eighty-calorie yogurt, Egg Beaters, and the last of the Ben & Jerry's Cherry Garcia. And hallelujah! In eight days I've lost four pounds! Maybe I should write a book about the MF diet. Lose all your money, lose weight—guaranteed! A best seller!

....

One night two of my Major Life Saver friends (MLS!), Barbara and Eric, phone and say, "We're on our way to take you to dinner—now!" I haven't been out once in the evening since I was "Madoff'd," as people are calling it.

As I button on a clean shirt, I start to visualize the MF, who has been parading around town with that rictus smile on his greedy bloated face while, back at his glam penthouse, his personal chef is sweating in one of the kitchens, preparing moist, exquisitely rare Kobe beef for him.

Eric and Barb arrive in what seems like two seconds, whisk me away from my visions and into their car, and take me to a small Greek restaurant. I can't believe how good real food tastes and how comforting it is to be out with dear friends.

I fall sound asleep the minute I hit my bed but wake up at four a.m. with the terrors beating down in full force. What is to become of me? What happens when I am old and wizened and can't take care of myself? What happens if I get sick, what if I'm diagnosed with something the next time I see the doctor? Paul would be there to comfort me but he's an artist, always struggling with financial miseries himself.

I start compulsively adding numbers, trying to figure out every cent I could make if I sell everything I have that's salable. I'll become the queen of Craigslist! Finally I give up on the math and brew a cup of coffee. It's not even six, but I head downtown to SoHo to start the day's work.

I still haven't said anything to Carmina. When I tell a friend of mine about Carmina and what she means to me, she says, "I'd rather give up my husband than part with Jolene, who's been with me eighteen years." I am not alone; these relationships run deep, and it's about much more than cleaning.

....

One Saturday night I lock the studio door behind me, and think, "Okay, enough of this work. It's time to treat yourself."

I call Paul and we decide we'll watch some TV and eat a pizza. There's a Domino's on my corner so I sally in and order two pies, no salads, no extras. When I hear the piped-in Christmas carols, a deep sadness overwhelms me. As a child I went to church almost every Christmas Eve with my grandmother. Just the two of us. We always sat in the left front pew so she could keep her eye on her old buddy, the archbishop, who was offering up the holy Mass. She knew almost everyone in the cathedral by name and I was proud to be with her in that sanctuary of pious persons.

"Keep your knees together, don't cross your ankles, sit up very straight," she would admonish me. The world seems so bright and full of promise when you're a child and there are gifts under the tree.

"Suck it up," I say to myself in Domino's, dragging myself back from that memory of happy anticipation. "Don't waste valuable time on self-pity." Time is money, and I no longer have all the time in the world.

The plain cheese and veggie feast pizzas smell delicious and are ready to go. But the tab comes to over $20!

"I thought the ads say, 'Buy one, get one free,'" I protest. That's why I ordered two!

"Only on Tuesdays," the cashier replies with a sympathetic nod. Are the rip-offs ever going to stop in this country? I pay for the two pies and leave, but that feeling of being tricked stays with me all night.

I wake up at 4:46—exactly—almost every morning now. Sometimes I take a tranquilizer to get back to sleep for a couple of hours but mostly I bolt out of bed as fast as I can, before the anxiety demons rev their engines, ready to mow me down emotionally.

This morning, though, I sit back on a tangle of pillows, with my steaming coffee in a Herend mug with its beautiful gold and deep red design. It better never break; I won't be able to afford another one. In a short while the rising sun will ricochet off the glass skyscrapers in the distance and my room with turn pale gold in the morning light.

How long will I be able to live here? Bob, my tax attorney and old friend, actually paid an emergency house call the day after the MF debacle and laid out some short-term plans.

"You're too traumatized to move," he advised. "Just assume you'll be staying here and let's revisit the situation in a few months. I know you. You'll make money again. I'm sure of it."

Bob's words and confident attitude helped restore in me a scintilla of calm. I was dead certain I'd have to find somewhere else to live—a dark, small, porcupine hole of a place— but at least now I have some time!

I must sell the little cottages in Florida and the Hamptons as soon as possible and pay back the loans. But I am one of many sellers looking to get rid of property in the middle of a recession. How long will it take for someone to buy them? What if no one does? Then what will I do? It's painful to part with places I've scraped and painted and furnished and made my own. But I cannot let myself become sentimental. I need money and they have some value.

I command my brain to SNT (Stop Negative Thinking)!

This takes an enormous effort of will but it's something I must do. Otherwise I'll just get paralyzed by the frightening reality of my situation. And I'll never leave this bed.

I'm in a beautiful apartment and I've lived a great and interesting life. I admit that I love beautiful things—high-thread-count sheets, old china, watches, jewelry, Hermès purses, Louboutin red-lipstick-soled shoes. I like expensive French milled soaps, good wines, and white truffles. With long years of steady work, I have been able to afford such things, and they've brought me pleasure. I have given extravagant gifts like diamond earrings and even a Rolex watch, and that has brought me pleasure, too. I've traveled a lot and loved every minute of it. In this past year, I've been to Laos, Cambodia, India, Russia, and most recently to Berlin for my first solo art show. Will I ever be able to explore exotic places again? Probably not.

Negative thinking again! Stop immediately! Self pity, too. Get over it!

I will myself to concentrate on the sun as it begins its magic, and as its rays transform my room I muse about the parts of my life that I am most proud of. About trying to better women's lives with the pink ribbon, about giving money to a friend's daughter to send her through college (no, she never knew it was from me), about secretly paying to have my mother's memoirs published (by a vanity press, but she never realized it), about the years I spent helping those who cannot read and mentoring retired schoolteachers, about helping friends and even strangers in any way I could.

I sit back and wish I'd done much more. I *will* do more, I will give more back, I vow, and it is this impulse that finally rouses me out of bed.

I've written two blogs for Tina and I've been paid for them. I have enough to last for only a few more months but the small check means *I can still earn money.*

I will need to find a job. But what? But how? Here's an idea: set up a lemonade stand on Worth Avenue in Palm Beach and charge a million bucks a glass, save a few dollars for myself, and give the rest to the charities that the MF wiped out. That thought elicits a chuckle. It feels so good to laugh. A sense of humor and a sense of the absurd are crucial in my situation. When Paul dropped by yesterday to check on how I was doing and saw me head down on the kitchen counter, he said, "Hey, you look a lot younger. Crying makes your face puffier, much better than Botox." He took me by the shoulders and said, "Don't lose your sense of humor. It's the only thing that will really get you through this."

In fact, I am not a weeper and have shed no tears over my situation. And yet when a friend wrote me yesterday about the death of her husband after a horrible illness, the e-mail undid me. There are so many worse things happening in the world—and I remind myself of this all the time—but still, each of us, no matter how bad things are for others, has his own worries, his own horror stories, especially now with the deepening economic turmoil.

I think of that grieving friend again for a few moments and I am surprised to realize that some good has come out of the MF debacle. I jot down a quick list of the positive aspects beginning to emerge from the horror of the experience:

> Agonizing but energizing
> Terrifying but clarifying
> Frightening but strengthening

And then I add:

> Weight loss from money loss!

....

The sun has vanished suddenly and the morning light has turned a most forbidding opaque gray. The windchill factor has fallen by a steep eighteen degrees. On my windowsill are four orchid plants. Three were gifts from friends and the fourth I bought a few months ago at the flower market on Twenty-seventh Street.

Those poor plants are living in the worst conditions, but I love them and talk to them like some sort of lunatic—this is what green thumbs recommend. The sill is freezing in the winter and hot as a pancake griddle in the summer. I water them from a pretty copper watering can, and feed them, but they never seem to blossom. What would, under such circumstances? But this morning, looking out at the moody gray city, I see a shoot with some unmistakable buds on it. My orchid will bloom again. I will see the pristine white flowers by the new year.

CHAPTER 5

Road Trip with "The Girls"

MF + 2 WEEKS

On a cold December day, I set out in my dented white '95 Mercedes wagon for Florida. I need to make sure my cottage is in shipshape order for a potential buyer. The newspapers have announced that the real estate market is worse in Florida than anywhere else in America and the broker who is trying to sell the place says, "The buyers are bottom feeders and they're all out for blood—if indeed there are any buyers at all." I will have to sell the tiny house for much less than I paid for it two years ago, not to mention that I will lose the money and effort I put into rejuvenating it from its previous trashy state. But no matter how much I lose, I must sell the little house. I need the cash for daily living.

I have an additional, more inspiring plan for my trip,

though. I want to take on-location photographs while I'm down south—it's emotionally crucial that I stay focused on my work.

Several years ago I began to photograph plastic blow-up sex dolls that come equipped with cavernous open mouths and huge breasts. The irony is that my work comments on insatiable consumerism, greed, dishonesty, and the deformed and warped values of our times. The dolls, with their gaping mouths, are symbols or ciphers that provide a visual scaffolding for social observation. Nothing in the pictures is genuine (unless you consider plastic "genuine") and neither, of course, was the MF.

Now "the girls," as I call them, are stacked in open wine cartons behind me, along with their wigs, clothes, lingerie, bags, shoes, gloves, and jewelry, all of which I bought on Canal Street in Manhattan—two bogus Hermès Birkins and a fake green Goyard bag, featherweight look-alike Rolexes and Panerais, spangle-laden bras, bikinis made of strands of edible plastic candy pearls. The tab for an afternoon's shopping for their sexy faux-luxe-brand dresses, bags, underwear, and rhinestone trappings has never topped eighty dollars.

Don't ask me where the idea of sex dolls came from. I am a nonkinky, heavily bourgeois kind of person. I had no interest in Barbie stuff when I was a kid. My best guess is that the dolls represent something deeply Freudian that is best left undisturbed. Or maybe it's more prosaic, maybe using the girls simply evolved from a bunch of weird, deformed children's dolls I photographed over and over in a dusty window in Rome when I was a visiting artist at the American Academy three years ago.

I-95 is a terrifically boring stretch of road and while I drive, my mind keeps slipping back to yesterday, when I finally had to tell Carmina that I was leaving the city to go down south to sell the cottage and that the MF had chopped my financial life into mincemeat.

We were standing in my kitchen after she'd just unfolded the ironing board.

"I can't have you here so often," I heard myself saying. "I just don't have the money. That guy took all my savings."

I burst into tears for the second time since December 11 and just kept hugging her sturdy shoulders as tightly as I could. She started crying, too.

"What will you do? Do you have enough money?" I asked, not even waiting for her to answer.

"I will pay you as much as I can," I said, having no idea where I'd earn my next dollar but knowing with certainty that somehow Carmina had to be part of my new frugal life. "Don't worry, I will still pay you—I'll find a way. Can you come for just a half day a week, or two mornings for a couple of hours?"

"Don't worry, Alexandra," she said through the tears, "I know about that guy from the newspapers and also TV. Everything will be all right. Really. You work very hard, you'll be okay. I'll be okay, too. Really."

"Let's sit down and have some coffee," I said and proceeded to heat up the espresso maker. Carmina had just finished a cup but she can drink endless amounts of dark brew.

I was relieved when she told me she had a new boyfriend who treated her well and she felt safe. She's a very brave woman and nothing gets her down. She's a role model of optimism and spunk and hard work. But I know her family is depending on her back in Bolivia.

"I'll make money," I said. "I'm even thinking I can write another book. And the art market has to revive someday. And I will never let you go. Unless you want me to."

"I would come even if you don't pay me, " she responded instantly. At those words I started crying again and even now, as I write this, tears come to my eyes. Carmina is blood-close and always will be. And I *will* find a way to pay her. There's no choice about this. Carmina will be employed by me as long as she is willing or until I call it a day. Learning what parts of my BMF (Before MF) life are indispensable is a process I now deal with daily, sometimes hourly.

I wish the radio or the old-fashioned cassette player in my car still functioned, because as I drive this silent, interminable highway, my mind begins to race with the same old scary thoughts. How am I going to survive? Was I greedy? No, I don't think so. Nine to ten percent interest was not disproportionate at that point in time. Maybe others wanted to strike it rich with the MF. I didn't. I just wanted financial stability, financial security, and the calming feeling that came from having my money in a safe place. I had lost money with other financial advisers, but the MF's fund, I was told, would yield a steady interest—not too high, not too low—allowing me to have a studio and work on my art. And the fund money, along with sales of my photographs, did support me for the past couple of years.

I think, as I often do, of the thousands of other Madoff

casualties. Many have far worse troubles than I. Some are very old and fragile and truly penniless, with not even a relative to turn to and with no conceivable way to make a buck. Some will be forced to leave their homes and what will happen to them? At least I've been told I can stay for the near future in my sunny apartment. You might expect that thinking about these poor souls would make me feel better, but somehow, perversely, it turns my own outlook darker and blacker and more self-absorbed. My fate may become their fate. You're going to lose your edge, I think, you'll be walking around with swollen ankles, you'll be holding your moth-eaten layers of old clothes together with rusted safety pins, your hair will be grayish yellow and dirty and stringy and you'll be cold and lonely and alone.

It's very clear I need to learn meditation immediately, because I just don't have the mental discipline to stop thinking obsessively about myself and about the future. I will check the Yellow Pages as soon as I reach my destination. Cars are murderously swerving in front of me as I hold to a steady 65 mph in the right-hand lane. I again try to concentrate only on driving, but my racing brain will not cooperate.

But wait, here's the worst thought of all: people are going to feel sorry for me. I can feel that pity right now, right here in my gut.

I don't want to feel like an object of pity, a damaged person who's marked down like a "second." This, I suddenly see, is what a real bag lady must feel like: a person who has no standing in society, a lone woman who trudges along with her ragged bags or pushes her creaky shopping cart with all her sad belongings. Where does she go to the bathroom? Where can she wash her hair? She has no place to call home. No place to cheer her. No one to love her.

No way is that going to happen to me! No effing way! I'll keep up appearances with my self-ironed white shirts and my self-applied nail polish (feet are no problem but I haven't quite gotten the hang of doing my right hand yet). And I will keep up my spirits and my belief in kindness and decency until I can't anymore and my soul starts to shred and shrivel—and then it will be time to call it quits. But not yet. Not by a long shot.

....

Eventually, the old dented wagon has carted me all the way to North Carolina and I pass several large peeling yellow-and-red-lettered road signs that advertise Café Risque in a hamlet called Dun, right off I-95. Café Risque! It's a topless bar/sex-shop/adult video place that offers "trucker showers." I have a huge urge to steer off the highway to investigate further. My mind has clamped onto a wild visual image of what trucker showers must look like. What a great location for the girls! I'm positive they would shine at their best in Café Risque. I pass the exit by, but am grateful for the temporary distraction.

The road is so straight and monotonous that, once again, my thoughts snap back to my life AMF (After MF). My brain replays the words a woman left on my answering machine a few days ago. She mumbled in an intimate semi-whisper, "I heard of your recent problems and would like to buy your jewelry."

Ugh! What a creepy message. I know generally what my stuff is worth—I was the only one who ever bought me earrings and rings and bracelets. I have a couple of good gold watches, also self-purchased, and I often sport a white Chanel J12 that was a gift from a generous girlfriend as a thank-you for some photographs I took of her children. I know exactly what I have and my jewels, however much I love them, don't add up to that much. For all I know, this jewelry-buying scheme may be part of a new Madoff family heist!

Another caller that same day, my friend Annette, left a message inviting me to a Christmas Day lunch in Palm Beach. When I RSVP'd "Love to!," I signed my e-mail with my new title, "AP, aka Person of Reduced Circumstances (PoRC)." As I continue to the long drive toward Florida, I think about Annette's party and about Palm Beach, which happens to have been the prime hunting ground where the MF went snouting for investor prey. People joined the Palm Beach Country Club where he hung out so they could be "invited" to join his exclusive enterprise.

This will be the first party I've attended since I was MF'd. Will people see me differently? Will I notice if they do? Should I bring a small Christmas gift, as I would have if this were last year? And what in the world would be appropriate for a PoRC to give for a hostess present? What will I wear? I try to remember what clothes I've packed for myself. Thank god! Finally, I'm thinking about something fun! I'd much rather waste time ruminating about wardrobe options than dwelling on bag lady fears.

My mind slows its anxious whirring and I begin to concentrate on driving. I don't go over the speed limit much—the old dented wagon wouldn't like it—but mostly I slow because if I am caught racing down the road with the girls in the back, I might land in the local clink, labeled a pervert, a kind of trouble I definitely don't need right now. And then I see the humor in it. With all the bags and boxes in the wagon, I'm a bag lady on wheels!

It's getting dark. I have to find a place to sleep. Signs have been whizzing by with motels advertising $29.95 and $39.95 a night. My friend Tom, an inveterate New York–Florida driver, and a man of swell taste, tells me that the finest hostelry on the route are Hampton Inns. All the hotel chains have well-lit franchises staked out immediately off I-95 exits so it's easy to find a Hampton Inn.

"Eighty-nine dollars," says the pleasant young lady at the desk when I inquire about a room. I, who used to buy only retail and have always been highly reluctant to bargain, ask for a discount. She takes it down ten bucks. For no reason. Just because I asked.

Although it's expensive compared to what is down the street, it isn't in the same solar system as the Ararat Park Hyatt in Moscow, where I was on a work project last year and where the rate for a single room was $2,100 per night. That number staggered me; I ended up at a fine place a few blocks away that charged a tenth of the Park Hyatt's rate.

I've stayed at a lot of ultrapricey hostelries, but who in their right mind would pay $2,100, except look-at-me-see-my-money oligarchs? I wouldn't be surprised if those

Gazprom guys and those other oligarchs had tons of rubles stashed away with Madoff. I keep thinking of Magritte's surreal paintings. My new meltdown world seems like a bizarre replica of what it used to be.

The Hampton Inn is my new Four Seasons! The room is warm and inviting with white duvets fluffed high on the king-size bed. There's even a polished maplewood board to rest in your lap so you can work on your computer in bed. There's no charge for wireless access, the pale beige stone sink is set into genuine granite, and the oversize white bath towels are extraheavy. The place is immaculate and breakfast is free! A sweet scent wafts down the hall and someone knocks on the door and offers freshly baked chocolate chip cookies. Can I be dreaming?

The aroma makes me realize I'm hungry. As I turned off I-95 I spotted a nearby Popeyes, my favorite fast-food place, and I head there now. Giggling youngsters are gulping down Coke from quart-size plastic cups. They eat the mashed potatoes and gravy with gusto. They gorge on biscuits that really are scrumptious but don't kids need protein and milk? The chicken is a bargain, $3.49 for three pieces (50 cents extra for a drink), but mostly the children leave their chicken untouched in the red plastic baskets. The parents don't seem to protest. Fast-food joints are the cheapest dining option— and the least healthy. Nonetheless I opt for a caloric binge and order two pieces of spicy fried chicken and a mountain of creamy coleslaw.

The buffet breakfast the next morning at the Hampton Inn has some more nutritious options. I load my tray with low-calorie yogurt, fresh fruit, and Special K. While the voices of TV hosts jackhammer over the soft Southern accents of the hotel's guests, I appraise the guests' butts. They are large, larger, huge. Mine is quite expansive, too, I must admit. I've spent a lifetime trying to control the spread; it's a combat that never ends.

These are nice folks, who smile and say "hi" as they microwave flour gravy to heap on the biscuits. The coffee in the large spigotted metal urns is labeled "robust," "regular," and "decaf." I take my first sip, and the coffee is already sweetened. More calories! No wonder people's butts are expanding.

After breakfast, I climb into the old wagon in another clean white T-shirt and I'm back on I-95 with four hundred miles to go. I wish I could chauffeur myself right over the horizon to China. I want to drive for the rest of eternity and never arrive anywhere. Arriving will mean reckoning with my future.

The miles zip radiolessly past; the girls seem content in the backseat. I took a few minutes this morning to slide some $10.99 Canal Street dresses on them to cover the sexy underwear they usually wear—just in case a state trooper happens to check out my cargo. Some of them are still in wine cartons, but the dressed-up ones are now stuffed, semi-deflated, into shiny shopping bags with old towels covering them. The bags will soon be tattered . . . but will be reused in my new life as a bag lady. The dark visions are back. Forget this meditation business, I need heavy-duty tranquilizers. I've brought my new prescription bottle with me but I'm still compos mentis enough to know it's not wise to partake of chemical serenity while driving.

Do I regret having put my savings in the MF's hands? I've lived by the premise that regret is a wasted emotion. After I left college and faced many major crossroads, I began to feel that whatever decision I made was the right one at the time that I made it, given that I always collected and analyzed as much information as I could about my options. I didn't want to leave any room for future regrets.

The decision to invest my money with the MF was the right one at the time that I made it. I did my homework. I sought out and talked with many informed people about Madoff and, with just one exception, they all agreed I was "safe" with him. I can't put my now wise self into my then innocent self. I don't blame myself for my losses. Loss is a part of living; I don't like it but I don't take it personally.

....

I finally arrive in Florida and, exhausted, fall into a troubled tossing-and-churning sleep. When I wake up in the morning, it's sunny, and it's Christmas Day. My little—but stylish— shack is on the wrong side of the tracks; this afternoon I am crossing over to Annette and Joe's for their holiday lunch in the luxurious environs of Palm Beach—the island, as the locals call it.

The luncheon is in an airy, casually elegant house with endless emerald green, close-cropped lawns; a cobalt-blue-tiled pool; and tall, slim, swaying—literally—royal palm trees. The food, prepared by the hosts' personal chef, is superb.

The dining tables are laden with white orchids, sparkling crystal, and old, heavy silver. I spot several large Warhols and some Schnabels on the walls.

I walk through the tall double doors made of aged pecky cypress, and Annette, the very soigné and beautiful hostess, a dear and empathetic friend, sees me right away and is just the same as she always is with me.

"It must be horrible to go through what's been happening to you," she says, handing me a flute of champagne, the first drink I've had since December 11, MF night.

"There are some people here you don't know," she says. "Come over and meet them." She steers me to a small group of guests who are laughing and sipping their icy champagne. As she's making the introductions, one of the women gives me the once-over, checking me out from my white Chanel ballet flats and J12 watch to my pearl earrings to my Kyle-at-Oscar-Blandi blond highlights. This is nothing new or Madoff-induced. Everybody knows that women check one another out all the time. Someone else in the group says, "Oh my god, you are the person that writes those blogs. A friend of mine e-mailed me one and I loved it." I acknowledge the nice words. They all want to hear about Madoff and how I knew him.

"Never met him," I explain, "but there are a ton of people here on the island who have lost huge fortunes with him." Of course, this group knows the Madoff story only too well, but I want to get the spotlight off me. I'm grateful when I hear a man who's holding a double shot glass of what appears to be straight vodka or gin say, "My wife and I had a lot of money with that bastard."

The group turns to him and starts pounding him with questions, and I'm able to slide away to talk with a couple of friends who've just arrived.

The butler whispers to our hostess that lunch is served. "It's buffet style," Annette says, "but look for your place cards so you know where you're sitting."

I'm situated next to the shot-glass man who has been Madoff'd, but now he says, "Not for so much money." He owns several houses and a "boat," which, down here, probably means a major yacht. No mention is made of having to sell any of the properties. Money is so relative, I think. I've got it easy compared to some people, and he has it easy compared to me. But I don't have time to sink further into these thoughts because my friend Joe, the host, who's on my other side, is so charming and funny. He's a great raconteur. It's pure pleasure to sit with another glass of champagne and listen. When everyone else is engrossed in conversations, Joe says quietly to me, "I know you'll be okay but if you ever need anything, just remember I'm a phone call away."

I'm overwhelmed by his words. All I can find to say is "I can't tell you how much that means to me," and I lift my glass to him.

I realize I'm having a great time. The Virginia Christmas ham is outrageously delicious, ditto the dripping-butter mac and cheese, the crisp haricots vert, the mâche salad, and the plethora of spectacular desserts. I take two helpings of everything, an unembarrassed three of the brandy-soaked plum pudding. For a minute I step outside myself and watch. I don't seem to have changed that much. I talk, I laugh, I listen. I've regaled my table with what it's like to write a controversial, highly personal blog, I've admitted some of my fears to my host but basically I'm just being me, broke, and having a good time with friends on a sun-washed Christmas Day. Until I wake up the next day at four a.m.

CHAPTER 6

Urgency at All Costs!

I can't remember how long I saved and went lunchless to buy an Hermès bag. It was the seventies and an Hermès Kelly cost about six or seven hundred dollars, which was almost a month's salary, but to climb the *Vogue* editorial ladder the bag was a necessity. And at *Vogue,* competition was exceedingly infectious; ascending the masthead quickly became an imperative.

I've always been ambitious. But I'm not competitive. Competitive, to me, means you have to win. For me, at the time, "competitive" was symbolized by the boarding school girls who battled on the hockey field at Smith. Those girls *had to win* even if it meant whacking someone in the shins with their sticks when they thought the coach wasn't looking.

I don't need to win at someone else's expense. But I'm

going to try as hard as I can at whatever I do. There's room for everyone, even at the top.

My job at *Vogue* included shuttling papers back and forth from the Promotion department to the publisher's office. At the time, the son of the owner of Condé Nast was the publisher of *Vogue*. In my mind I referred to him as the Boss of Bosses. He wore blue chambray shirts and gray sleeveless Shetland cardigans with brown leather buttons and never had his shoes on. His office was a third the size of Miss G's and his secretary worked in his office at a desk less than a dozen feet from his.

He had a great sense of humor and was a rare combination of informal and seemingly unapproachable. But I was never intimidated by him. One day, a book I had recently finished was lying on his desk in the spot where I normally deposited the copy for him.

"I just read that book," I said to him.

"I did, too," he responded, after a long pause during which he did not look up from his ubiquitous yellow pads, always full of numbers. Another uncomfortably long stretch of time passed and he added, "What did you think of it?"

We talked for about thirty seconds at most. The conversation ended: he thought the book was mediocre. I disagreed.

Over the weekend, while my son was napping, I started thinking about all the things I believed could be done to improve *Vogue* magazine. Impulsively I typed out—nonstop—a memo to the publisher with four single-spaced pages of ideas for stories for *Vogue*. The next time I delivered some papers to him, I said that I'd written him a memo, while clutching it in my hand. Without looking up, he motioned me to put it in the in-box.

The next day, after I dropped off more copy for him, he asked, "Do you have any more ideas where those came from?"

"Yes, many," I replied, trying to look as unemotional as he always appeared to be. He said nothing and never raised his eyes from the numbers scrawled in black felt-tip pen on his yellow legal pads. I was pretty sure I had overstepped my bounds.

A week later, I received a summons from Personnel.

"Please do sit down," said the personnel director, Mary Campbell. If people were frightened by Miss G, they were absolutely terrified of Miss Campbell. Even the Boss of Bosses was said to be on his guard around her.

She directed me to a down-filled loveseat upholstered in navy blue velvet. I sank into it and stared down at the chinoiserie rug, as something in me sensed it would be rude to look directly at her. Was I in trouble for writing that memo? Oh god, what had I been thinking? She rose from her desk and sat herself in a comfortable wing chair upholstered in deep blue silk. She looked at me and I looked at the gleaming antique English walnut coffee table upon which all of the Condé Nast magazines had been carefully fanned, *Vogue* occupying the top position.

"Would you be at all interested in being the beauty editor of *Glamour* magazine?" she asked. I looked up at her perfect platinum coiffure and straight into her stormy, blue-gray eyes. I didn't quite comprehend what she was saying.

She must have meant to say did I want to be an assistant to the beauty editor. Why was someone with such an important position offering me an assistant's job at a less prestigious magazine on a lower floor when I was a full-fledged promotion editor at *Vogue*? This was my comeuppance for writing that memo.

"Do you have any questions?" she asked, unsmiling, assuming I had said "yes" when I hadn't uttered one word. I replied that I did not have any questions at all and she said, "You'll see the editor in chief this afternoon at three, and if all goes well, you can start tomorrow."

It sounded urgent. I understood urgency. I nodded and said I'd be there. When Miss C issued an order, the only choice you had was to obey. By five that afternoon, *Glamour*'s Publicity department had called me to read the corporate release announcing that I was to be the new beauty editor of *Glamour*, Condé Nast's largest and most financially successful magazine. That was when I finally comprehended what had transpired in Miss C's office, and I was in a state of complete mind-body shock. I was to be responsible for producing forty or more editorial pages a month. I soon learned that I was also to receive an enormous salary raise and not one but *two* assistants.

Everything at Condé Nast happened *in a flash*.

I was overwhelmed as I whipped up dinner for my son and husband that evening. Rick suggested we toast my new job with a glass of wine. It took me a moment to register what he was saying and to raise my glass. Things had happened with such speed that the day seemed completely unreal.

The next morning I agonized about what to wear. What did a *Glamour* beauty editor look like? Beauty? I personally was no beauty but I knew I had to look good. Very good, very "pulled together," which was the high compliment I had received from *Vogue* fashion editors on the occasions when I met their enigmatic standards.

Finally I pulled on a khaki Saint Laurent top from Rive Gauche, with matching khaki pants—a major splurge even at the discount price that *Vogue* editors often received—and checked my black Hermès Kelly purse in the mirror to see if it looked right with the outfit. I wished I had a sportier bag—maybe a Gucci hobo, which Miss G carried when she was in her "casual" traveling outfit (a seven-eighths length leopard coat, Galanos gray-flannel jumpsuit, and mid-heeled chocolately brown shoes, made to order in Paris), but in truth the Kelly was the only decent bag I owned.

I strode purposefully into my new office. It was even larger than Miss G's. The company decorator was waiting and asked me what "look" I wanted. There was no time to think—there never was at Condé Nast. So I said, with all the authority I didn't feel, "Just white. All white. Please."

By the end of the week, I was ensconced behind two sparkling titanium white Parsons tables, with three white slipper chairs done up in white canvas for guests. The assistants each had a smaller Parsons table and *their* assistant had one, too, along with their own canvas-covered chairs.

I'd always loved Miss G's white orchids so I wrote a polite memo to the decorator asking for a plant for each table. A few hours after the memo was delivered—everything was done lickety-split, chop-chop for chief editors—my office was festooned with white pots each bearing four or five stems of blooms, a bit over the top for my taste but who was I to say no? My entire new environment, indeed the air the assistants and I breathed, was superchic. Only three years ago I was in jeans every day gallivanting with my husband across Europe in a small car with no destination. Now I was sitting in this large fancy office and I had to figure out a way to generate forty intelligent and visually arresting editorial pages tout de suite. I didn't know what else to do but affect an aura of urgency and an efficient, knowing manner. The whole facade peeled off the second I hit home and started stirring pasta for my son and husband's dinner.

CHAPTER 7

There *Is* Such a Word as "No"

My assistants at *Glamour* were holdovers from the previous editor, who had been an imperious Miss G type. They were well-trained in the "there is no such word as 'no'" school. They approached my table with long lists of meetings to attend and people to interview. My editor in chief, the fabled Ruth Whitney, had left me with the advice, "You'll learn by doing and I have complete faith in you." I didn't have the foggiest idea where her trust came from. Maybe my *Vogue* memo had been passed on to her to convince her that at least I had some fresh ideas.

My first face-to-face was with the Viennese art director, Mrs. D. The bosom buddy of the previous beauty editor, Mrs. D clearly didn't think I had the goods to replace her friend. I wasn't sure I did, either.

"We need to do a bath story," she stated the minute I entered her office. Like Miss G, she never absented her space except to okay layouts. Unlike Miss G's leopard lair, Mrs. D's office had a sterile air with its centrally placed long work-table and its single drawing pad. An overhead spotlight was aimed at the pad and two highly sharpened pencils in a chrome holder lay nestled next to it. It reminded me of an operating room.

We need to do a story? Hmmm, wasn't it the beauty editor's job to come up with story ideas? At least that's what they did at *Vogue*.

"I would like to see a ravishing nude in a beautiful bath-tub in an even more beautiful bathroom," she continued in a heavy Austrian accent, not leaving me a second to utter a word. She focused on the pad in front of her and pencil-sketched—poorly—her vision.

"The photographer is Gianni Luttini," she finished, handing me her sketch and placing the pad to one side of her desk. I knew I was dismissed when she started sorting other papers into perfect piles. I had my marching orders. I almost clicked my heels together before making an obedient second lieutenant's turn out of her office.

I'd been on several shoots for *Vogue,* so I had at least some inkling of how to proceed. When I called Luttini, who was famous for being difficult, to schedule the shoot, Mrs. D had already done it—for the next day.

He informed me that he needed "the most *perfect* bathroom in New York," and "a model with a *perfect* body." He spoke mostly in Italian, but I recognized the gist of a command when I heard one.

I was to organize the entire shoot within the next twenty hours.

There is no such word as "no."

I found the perfect bathroom. A friend of mine's rich grandmother had an amazing one with a Pissarro on the wall opposite the sink. (I was told it was authentic but didn't they understand—or care—that the humidity would completely ruin the painting?) My assistants located the perfect model. Little did I know that under no condition would she take off her clothes. I was also unaware that *Glamour* magazine didn't countenance nudes in its pages. The Viennese Viper had set me up!

My first shoot at *Glamour* was, of course, a disaster. Although she didn't let on, the editor in chief knew full well that Mrs. D had a history as a troublemaker. She was kind enough never to ask to see Luttini's pictures. I think he probably didn't have film in his camera anyway.

....

Over the course of my four years at *Glamour,* I endured several more of the Viennese Viper's ideas for stories. One of them involved a trip to the Caribbean with a famous French photographer whom the VV had flown over first class on the Concorde from Paris the week before. He was a tall, overweight, distinctively ugly man with a kind of Nixon-like demeanor with wobbly, just-forming jowls. He never looked me straight in the face while making demands in his heavy French accent.

Three models; a hairdresser; his assistant; a makeup artist and her assistant; the photographer and his assistants; my assistant, P; and I trooped down to St. Maarten to shoot a major bathing suit portfolio for the March issue. I had scheduled five days, which was a long stretch to be away from my family, but this was, according to the VV, a "most important portfolio" and therefore required an unusual amount of time.

The French photographer turned out to be a maniac. Nothing I could do or say or provide was okay for him. The food (not French), the rooms (which were lovely), the hairdresser (one of the best), the clothes (edited by him), even the models (also chosen by him) were ruthlessly criticized. Within two days I'd had it with the whiny, moody creep.

I'd been driven to the point that I didn't care if we had no pictures to show the VV.

I didn't care if I was fired.

I told P that I was stopping the shoot after lunch on the fourth day and I would book return tickets for all of us. I asked her if she could handle the shots that had already been planned for the morning.

P said calmly that she could cope with the French photographer and that she could get the necessary pictures.

"Okay, I'm not letting you utter another word," I said. "If you really believe you can take over, I will depart on the next plane." And I did. It was the first and only time I left a shoot before it was done.

There was a lesson here for me: there *is* such a word as

"no." And although, to paraphrase the legendary *Vogue* editor Diana Vreeland, "'No' means elegance," "no" can also mean "no fucking way." The French photographer was unreasonable and professionally out of his mind and I was fed up with him—and with the Viennese Viper as well.

I weighed the situation carefully in my room that night. I didn't think I would be fired—I hadn't been in the job long enough for my boss to think I was a complete catastrophe as an editor—but obviously I was willing to risk it. If I were let go, I would find another job at another magazine company or I'd freelance. The decision would be the right one because I had fully dissected the options.

A few days later P returned to New York. I did not know—and did not ask—how she did it, but she brought back enough pictures for a beautiful twelve-page portfolio. Today P is one of the most successful, most sought-after stylists in the business.

A few weeks later, I left my white office at *Glamour* and went to pick up my son at nursery school on Lexington Avenue at Eighty-first Street. As I walked from the subway I passed the brightly lit Rosedale Fish Market. A small hand-lettered sign in the window advertised HELP WANTED. I didn't need to be at school for another twenty minutes, so, on a whim, I ducked in and asked the cashier about the job.

"You have to speak to Robbie, the owner," she said, pointing at a tall red-faced man in a white apron expertly carving fillets out of an enormous pink salmon.

He wiped his hands on the towel that was folded over his apron strings and strode over to the cash register. We talked for less than five minutes and he offered me a job as daytime cashier. I took it on the spot. He said that I could read books if the store wasn't busy. Three days a week I would have four hours off to attend the Art Students League, where I'd always wanted to go to learn how to draw.

I had been trying to come up with a plan to leave *Glamour* since the disastrous trip to St. Maarten, and for god knows what reason, it had all gelled in the instant I walked into the fish market. My strategy was to work at Rosedale, to try my hand at freelance writing, to attend the Art Students League, and to apply to graduate school for a master's degree in Studio Art.

I picked up my son, and I was more thrilled than usual with the finger paintings he bestowed upon me as a present. I'd bought some fresh swordfish at Rosedale (from now on I would get a major discount there) and I cooked it with lemon and dill. Our son ate his dinner first, and we read him two Babar stories, and then two more. We hugged and kissed him good night and in a few minutes he fell asleep, a true angel with his fine hair golden from the light in the hallway.

My new gig would give me much more time to be with him. With two emotionally distant parents, I was often on my own as a child. I didn't want my son's childhood to be that way. There'd be no more packing of Paris-bound Vuittons deep into the night. No more nightmares about Viennese Viper art directors. The chichi life of Condé Nast had become too rich for my blood. The endless business lunches, the many nights spent at charity or industry dinners instead of with my family, had become meaningless. I began to see my closetful of designer clothes as reflecting the superficiality of the fashionable world that I inhabited by day. I couldn't care less if I never ate another baked potato with shaved white truffles—a favorite of mine at the Four Seasons restaurant, where I had been allotted my own table. I wrote down a list of reasons why I was leaving:

> Your children are only young once.
> Live the life you want to live, not the one
>   you're supposed to live.
> Follow your big dreams while you are able
>   to do so.
> New experiences are what make life
>   interesting.
> Listen to your heart as well as your head.
> Try something unexpected and adventurous—
>   you can always go back to what you
>   did before.

I went to my bookshelf and took out a worn green cloth-covered college edition of Thoreau and added this quotation to my list:

> "If one advances confidently in the direction of his dreams and endeavors to live the life which he has imagined, he will meet with a success unexpected in common hours."

After dinner that night, over decaf espresso, I told my husband about my new job. To his enormous credit, he didn't flinch. Perhaps he thought I was a bit tetched in the head, and he didn't have time to realize that I would go from a cushy editorial job to fishmongering, but I was his son's mother and that was really what counted. I told him my plans and that I was sure I could supplement my salary by doing some free-lance writing, since I'd made a lot of contacts at *Glamour*. I also said that if he thought this was a really stupid idea, all I had to do was tell Rosedale Robbie that I had changed my mind.

"No," he said, "I think I understand where you're headed."

I was so grateful for his support that tears came to my eyes.

The next day I told *Glamour*'s editor in chief that I was quitting to go back to school and to freelance. She sent out an afternoon memo to the staff: "AP is leaving for her own interesting reasons but I am sure she'll be back." Those weren't the exact words but they're pretty close.

Was I crazy to leave a high-paying, prestigious editorial job for a fish market? I don't think so. I knew that the longer I stayed at *Glamour*, the more unlikely it was that I would become an artist. Now that I look back and remember the big chance I took in my twenties, becoming a fishmonger in order to pursue my dreams, I think surely I can find a way out of the mess I'm in now.

CHAPTER 8

The Copy Shop Collapse

MF + 4 WEEKS

It's been four weeks since the Madoff bomb detonated into my life. I'm back in New York. The Florida house is still for sale. The cottage on Long Island is also on the market. No takers, or even lookers, for either house.

I've now written three blogs. Ed Victor, my agent, thinks he might be able to sell a book based on them. Despite childhood ambitions, I've never considered myself a writer or an author. I've written books as a working journalist, and I know that my strength is ideas, not sentences. My idea is to write about what happens when one's worst nightmare comes true.

On a Monday, I hear the judge has once again given the MF a get-out-of-jail-free card, and I can't stand it. I was brought up believing in the American system of justice and that what the judge says goes. The MF gamed the system for all it was worth and the same system seems to be protecting him. Luckily, as I am visualizing him, wolfing down a gourmet dinner in his dandy penthouse, I am at the Four Seasons in New York dining on risotto laced with black truffles. My friend RP e-mailed me earlier in the day: "Last minute idea: do you want a FREE dinner that will help save the earth?" Who am I to turn down a free meal at the Four Seasons, under *any* circumstances?

During the cocktail hour I notice, among the ladies, a conspicuous lack of the large stones that glittered with such delicious abandon in premeltdown days. I pay special attention because the other day I received another phone message about selling my jewels. This time it was from one of the big auction houses. A polished voice asked if I would like a "complimentary consultation on how to discreetly dispose of your jewels."

Excuse me, where did anyone get the idea I have such valuable gems? I wish!

I meet RP at the venerable Grill Room, where I had countless business lunches as a high-flying magazine editor. The government of Malaysia is sponsoring a dinner for the first Earth Awards, and finalists from all over the globe talk about how they have been working for years to help the planet. In the beneficent atmosphere, I forget about the MF and news tidbits about his wife paying for his security guards and fat cigars—with whose money? Okay, maybe I don't forget entirely.

....

I arrive home from the Four Seasons feeling wiped out from the day. I take a Tylenol PM and try to fall asleep. Another Tylenol and a tranquilizer three hours later don't do the trick and the demons do a shock and awe attack. Tonight, drugs don't help.

I contemplate the advice of my dinner partner that day, a doctor whose specialty is integrative medicine. I told him I was looking for someone who would help me with meditation, and asked if I would become addicted to the tranquilizers I take when I feel panicky. He said I didn't appear to have a problem yet. (When you become a PoRC, you grab any freebie advice you can get.) He suggested a book about yogic breathing exercises. Learning how to inhale and exhale is pretty far down my to-do list, but maybe I'm fooling myself about what will really help me fight the panic. Tomorrow I will find the book. It's been quite a while since I locked eyes with the lions in front of the New York Public Library on Forty-second Street. That's a good thing about being a PoRC, you get to have experiences that you forgot about when, for instance, it was easier just to one-click and order a book from Amazon.

....

I have until March 4 to file a claim for the SIPC insurance money that may be paid to people who've been swindled by the MF. SIPC says it can pay up to $500,000, but my savings were in an IRA (Individual Retirement Account) so it's not clear whether I will receive any remuneration at all. And if the government classifies me as the victim of a theft, and worthy of its largesse, how long will it be before I see the SIPC money? Six years? Eight years? By then, I figure, I won't need to have my hair colored; it will be a perfectly elegant shade of pure-panic white.

The morning after the Four Seasons dinner, I descend into the dark depths of the basement storage area of my apartment building to locate the MF's statements. I need to collect reams of materials in order to file the SIPC claim. Three hours later I'm covered with filthy dust but in my hands are all the documents going back to 1999, when I first put my money into the MF's funds.

The IRS instructs us to keep records for seven years, and I've dutifully complied. I throw out as much as possible because I have very little room for storage and neat-freak is embedded into my DNA. But for some reason—and I think it's because I'm always so worried about money—I have not thrown out one stub of the official-looking statements that the MF sent every month.

The pile is over a foot high and the papers weigh as much as two gold bricks. I must Xerox the stuff so I can give it to Bob, who is helping me with the SIPC forms.

Bob is a godsend. He's the attorney who paid a house call to me in what seems like a lifetime ago, with the heartening news that I could stay in my apartment for the time being. When he offered to help with all the paperwork, I hastened to tell him to please keep track of his hours. I will pay him of course (from what, I'm not sure), but he waved me off and said, "You don't have to worry about that."

I *do* worry. Of course I want to pay him for his advice and his hard work. I don't want to be a charity case for anybody, but I am extremely grateful for his smarts and his time. I can offer to do portraits of his grandchildren, but that's not nearly enough. I have to believe that my luck will change, and when it does, I will be able to pay him.

Three hours of my day so far have been spent on Madoff. I take a long, hot shower to get rid of the grime under my fingernails, and then get ready to head to Kinko's, where I'll copy the hundreds of pages of paperwork. Resentment wells up in me: for the time that has been spent, for the money that will be spent, for my dirty clothes and bad mood—all to have these effing Madoff forgeries copied.

The only way I can manage the loathsome stack of papers is to take a taxi to the shop: I use even more precious dollars than expected because we get mired in bad traffic.

At the copy shop, I stand in line watching the clock. Eighteen minutes tick by. Finally I am facing a young clerk with fancifully decorated, false clawlike fingernails. They are true works of fine art. And, it turns out, so is she.

I show her the pile and explain that I need two copies of each, collated, please.

"They are legal size and regular letter size," she tells me.

"Yes, they are," I agree.

"And some are double-sided," she says, rifling through the

sheets with the fingernails carefully pointed upward so they are not sullied by touching the paper.

"That's true," I say.

"I don't think we can do this job," she says, and begins to turn to the next customer.

"Can you tell me why not?" I say, trying to remain civil.

"There's nobody here who knows how to do this kind of job right now."

"Okay, I have some time on this, at least a couple of days," I say, knowing that I simply cannot lug this pile back to my apartment. "When will somebody who knows how to do this job be here?"

She is looking past me now, ready to help the person behind me.

"You'll have to speak to the manager," she says, not looking at me. Her cell phone rings. She answers and begins to talk.

Now I'm angry. But the copying must be done.

The manager is on his break, and there is no assistant manager on the premises. I run down the list of all my friends in offices who could let me use a Xerox machine. Out of the question: I can't impose on them for something like this.

It's now raining heavily outside. I have this big canvas bag of papers and nothing to protect them from the torrents. For a few seconds I stand there stupidly, not knowing what to do. I hail a taxi and give my home address.

Back in my apartment, I sit on my bed and give in to a ferocious rage that I haven't felt since it all happened. I try to cry but no tears come. I walk into the kitchen, then back to the bedroom, at least a dozen times. I open the fridge, look-ing for something to eat. I open and close the fridge door ten times or more. At last, I take out a yogurt, then smash it so viciously into the sink that the plastic container explodes onto every surface it can possibly cling to except the ceiling. Cleaning it up helps to calm me a bit.

I try to cry angry tears again, but no dice. I think of making myself a drink the way they do in the movies. But I would just get a headache. Finally, I find myself in the bath-room taking the longest, hottest shower of my life.

What do I really want to cry about? I ask myself. There are people far worse off than I am. I have my health. I have my wonderful but faraway son and my beloved niece and their amazing families. I have close friends who love and sup-port me in every way imaginable. I am not a bag lady—yet. Okay, I'm no spring chick, but I have some talent. I have connections. I am still sitting in this beautiful apartment. So I have to sell some stuff. So I have to go out and earn money again. So what?

I am actually talking out loud to myself. Reluctantly I leave the shower and the pelting water, which does seem to give me a measure of composure.

The phone is ringing and it's my friend Patty Marx. I tell her about the copy shop claw-nail clerk and how I came home and completely lost it.

"You're not angry at that girl, it's obviously about Madoff," she says, and of course I agree.

"Sure, you can always say people are worse off but it's not that meaningful or consoling, because it's happening to *you.* Just because things could be worse doesn't mean you have to be grateful for everything you have. What happened to you is real. It is bad," she says. "You were robbed. Allow yourself to be angry and pissed as much as you want."

We make a date to meet at EJ's for dinner the following week. I hang up and feel a huge relief. She's absolutely correct that no matter how often I rationalize that it could have been worse or think about the people for whom it was or is worse, I still have to contend with what happened to me. My whole body feels lighter after talking to her. Words help. Love and friendship help more than anything.

I am brushing my teeth that night when I think about what's worse than losing all your money:

> Losing your child or your husband or someone
> you most deeply love
>
> Losing your health
>
> Losing your mind
>
> Losing your sense of humor—maybe!

CHAPTER 9

Change Is Good:
My Fishmonger Days

Irish fisherman sweaters are aptly named—they were part of the garb of choice at Rosedale Fish Market. The oils retained by the natural woolen yarn foil the fragrance of the merchandise. Also essential was a lightweight rubber apron wrapped around your entire body so that it covered your jeans or OshKosh overalls. A clean white cotton apron topped that for hygienic purposes. Black rubber boots with salmon-colored soles had to be tall enough to reach under the apron. Thus your entire personage was shielded from unwanted scents and you could tread safely across the floors that were splashed with fresh water hourly to keep Rosedale spotlessly clean. I considered it a rather stylish uniform.

At Rosedale, I had plenty of time to read and study. Our

major traffic was in the early-morning hours, when private cooks came in to check out the catch of the day, and around four thirty to six in the late afternoon, when people were returning home from work.

Rosedale had always been hospitable to artists and writers and musicians, I learned. Robbie's wife came from a well-known, wealthy family. What Mrs. Robbie was doing in a fish market—albeit a very upscale one—I haven't the vaguest clue. But then again, I was there, too. Robbie took a shine to me and bestowed upon me the ultimate gift: I was allowed to be the first female to accompany him to the Fulton Fish Market.

Once a week, at four thirty in the morning, he would pick me up in his truck and we would barrel downtown. After he had bought the fish for the day, we'd head to a mahogany-paneled bar with beautiful old mercury-backed mirrors on the corner of South Street, where all the out-of-town fishermen in their baseball caps and heavy red-and-black-plaid mackinaw jackets hung out and tossed down their morning beer. Robbie would order a coffee and I would be perched on a tall stool, next to him, my rubber boots just skimming the shining brass floor rod. Robbie and the truck would scoot me home in time to take my son to school, then I'd circle back to the fish market for the day's work.

It was easy to slip into class at the Art Students League in my Rosedale outfit, as it looked rather outré and artistic, and the other students could never smell a thing—or at least they never said anything to me about it.

I had, as planned, applied to graduate school for further

study in painting. Yale was my first choice, but Hunter was in my neighborhood and I could attend afternoon seminars with Robbie's blessing and still have free nights to be with my family.

When a cosmetics company I knew from my days at *Glamour* called and asked me to work on a project as a consultant, I knew I had to quit Rosedale—I couldn't walk into the tony offices in the General Motors building where they were headquartered in my fishy clothes. I reluctantly left Rosedale after almost a full year. But I was thrilled about the money I was being paid for the cosmetics project and by the prospect of an untethered life as a freelance writer and fledgling artist.

Without a day job, I wanted to move downtown to a loft where I could have a studio to paint in. Pragmatically I knew it would never work because my son was in school on West Seventy-seventh Street, and living downtown would be an enormous hassle for all of us. I came up with the idea of renting a cheap loft for weekends instead of renting a house in the country and convinced my husband it would be fun.

I had met an artist at a cocktail party who lived in an area of town I didn't know anything about. He told me about his loft south of Houston Street in lower Manhattan. I didn't know exactly what a loft consisted of but I was curious, so I pulled on my well-washed Rosedale OshKosh coveralls and biked downtown one afternoon for a cup of tea.

He had an enormous white-painted space in a redbrick five-story walk-up with high ceilings and several skylights. In other words, a loft. The glossy floors were painted a neutral gray, and a black wood-burning cast-iron stove, the only source of heat, commanded the living space. Water for shaving and bathing was warmed up in a huge pot on a two-burner stove. The area where he worked was splattered with a brightly colored bouquet of oil paints and the walls were covered with tacked-up preliminary charcoal sketches. Here was the genuine *la vie Bohème*. It was three miles and universes away from my Upper East Side apartment, and I was instantly seduced.

I used any spare time I could find to hunt for a space, preferably in a cast-iron building on one of the neighborhood's cobblestone streets. I pestered supers and tracked down landlords to see what was available. I finally found a great open loft with wooden ceilings and tall windows on LaGuardia Place, which later became part of now-famous SoHo. My husband pitched in to whitewash the floor and all the walls, and we moved some mattresses, tables, and bikes in.

Our little family sometimes stayed at the loft on weekends and I painted as much as I could. I even threw a birthday party for my son there and all the uptown kids were wildly excited that they could roller-skate indoors. After a year the lease was up and my husband wanted to try something else. He had found some property in Vermont and designed a lovely shingled Cape Cod house for us to live in. We began heading north on weekends.

....

My husband and I very slowly drifted apart. I had loved my time downtown and wanted more of it. He preferred the New

England house. I preferred the city. I hated the five hours spent driving to Vermont and the five-hour return on Sunday nights. For me, it was a huge waste of valuable time that I could use to do things with my son or study and paint.

We began to spend long periods away from each other. When my son was at camp in Maine, I would take vacations there and paint the rocks and the ocean, while my husband stayed in Vermont. We had differing outlooks on life. I wanted adventure. I wanted to meet exciting people, to learn as much as I could, to have new experiences. He wanted the peace and tranquillity of his own home in the beautiful Vermont countryside.

At a dinner party recently, a young man whose parents had divorced in the early eighties during the postfeminist period, as my husband and I did, said, "My parents split up, and a lot of my friends' parents did, too; it seems as if it was the trendy thing to get a divorce in those years."

If you pressed me about exactly why my husband and I decided to go our separate ways, I couldn't give you a specific answer. Several of my friends were leaving their marriages and they reported feeling liberated and relieved without their conjugal responsibilities. I wanted a different kind of life and was intent on having it. Ours was a mutual agreement and mostly an amicable one. We separated but didn't divorce for almost six years. We remained close friends and we both wanted to make sure it was the right thing to do for us and for our son. The single most difficult, most painful moment of my life was telling my son that his father and I were separating. He was twelve at the time.

My now ex-husband found an elegant but smaller apartment adjacent to Fifth Avenue, a block away from where we had lived on Seventy-second Street. Our son would stay with him whenever he wanted to be uptown. I shed my Park Avenue self and rented a small, inexpensive interim one-bedroom on the outskirts of Greenwich Village that I found in the *Times* Classified section. The loft on LaGuardia Place, although still available, was way out of my new budget.

Of course I was plenty worried about money. These weren't bag lady fears; these were fears that came from being a mother, with a primary responsibility to be a good parent. I believed that feminist fairness called for me to pay half of my son's private school tuition and to contribute as much as I could for his food and clothing. My husband, who still had his job as an industrial designer, would give us as much as he could for child support. If we didn't have enough, we would apply for a scholarship so that our child could go to his uptown school without interruption. Separation and living downtown in a dramatically different style, away from his friends, was an enormous upheaval for a child. Our son needed as much familiar continuity as possible. Throughout this period, I was convinced that even if I had to work four jobs and sell Avon cosmetics door to door, I would make enough money to start a new kind of life.

And that is how I feel—most of the time—these days. I *will* do it. I will earn enough money so that I won't become a bag lady. I'm not sure exactly how but I will make it happen. I will write; I will make art. I will set up a Web site. I will create something that will bring in money. When the demons stage a full-scale assault, I yell at myself that I *can* do it—over and over again. And I convince myself. And I *will* do it.

Although I painted the new living quarters white, they were a major comedown from our uptown home with its spacious living room and stone fireplace, its formal dining room, and its large windowed kitchen. On most weekends my son would head to Vermont with his dad and then my place seemed pretty grim. I was lonely and uprooted but I kept my spirits up by thinking, This is all my own and I'll find something great as soon as I'm more settled financially.

I slept in the living room, my son had the bedroom, and every day we made a game of the long subway trip uptown to his school. I would drop him off and head back to look ceaselessly for a better and larger space so I would have room to work. Lofts abounded but they all needed "fixing," which meant painting the walls, putting in lights, bathrooms, and kitchen—installing everything needed for a bare-minimum existence.

I couldn't afford to pay "key money" for the lofts that were available with the basic improvements. Looking for a place to live was, as it always is in New York, a discouraging process. I went street by street, building by building, asking supers, owners, artists, anyone I could collar, if they knew of space for rent. I thought I was running my life, but then I realized real estate was completely in control. It was a depressing time. Often on weekends, when my son was away, I would lie in bed for hours and not want to eat or move. Finally I heard from a building owner that a small-job electrician might want to rent a space on West Broadway. The gallery scene was just beginning to flourish and SoHo's wonderful cast-iron buildings were about to be developed by uptown real estate barons. The wide street was in a central location and, most important, it was safe.

It wasn't a loft, it wasn't an apartment, but it was perfect. It had been a small outbuilding on a farm a hundred years ago. Two floors, each one far smaller than my uptown living room, were newly painted with titanium white walls. The kitchen was made for very small people: it measured less than five feet square, but it had a window. All in all, it was about six hundred square feet. The rent was $350 per month, not including electricity. In addition, Irwin, the landlord and electrician, wanted a security fee of $475.

I didn't have the money but I desperately wanted the place. P, my assistant from the days of the French photographer shoot, happened to be with me when the electrician had shown me the space. She offered to lend me the money. It was the first and last time I have ever accepted a loan. But she was gracious and insistent, and I wanted the place so much that I took her up on it. I paid her back, fifty dollars a month plus a tiny bit of interest, over the next year.

My son and I and our Norwegian elkhound, Pookabee, moved in. I adored the creaky steps, the uneven wooden floors, and the windows that looked onto the night-and-day industrial busyness of West Broadway. We had no furniture to speak of, as I had paid the last of my savings for a bed and bookshelves for my son, who had a room of his own.

I rented a huge industrial floor-sanding machine and

shined up the old wood, then cleaned and waxed and scrubbed until the entire place was as spotless and gleaming as I could make it.

Metropolitan Lumber was around the corner and they gave me a great deal on some unusable wooden doors and sawed them to size at no charge. I sandpapered, painted, and painstakingly gold-leafed them, and then devised a way to install them as sliding panels on the windows so we had privacy at night. I slept on a mattress on the floor next to my son's room, and organized my paints and canvas rolls and stretcher bars on the floor below.

Every morning after I returned from taking my son to school, I stood at the window of my sweet small space on West Broadway, where I could watch the famous painter Alex Katz walking down my street with his black dog, its tail wagging nonstop. I was on my way to becoming a genuine artist. But I needed money. The cosmetics project had come to an end. I had to pay for half of my son's school tuition plus rent, gas, electricity, food, phone, subway fare, my own tuition at graduate school, and art supplies.

I decided to call Alexander Liberman, an artist and sculptor as well as the legendary editorial director of Condé Nast. While I was at *Glamour* we often discussed the art scene, and I had told him about wanting to be a painter full-time.

When I phoned his office, his secretary remembered me and gave me an appointment to show him slides of my paintings. He didn't end up furthering my career as an artist, but he did something that was more crucial for me at the time. Mr. Liberman offered to pay me a thousand dollars a month as a "roving editor" for *Vogue*. My responsibilities were light: a meeting once a month where I would present ideas that other editors could produce, and one written article with any shoots necessary to illustrate it. It was a perfect job!

A guaranteed twelve thousand dollars a year was good money but not nearly what I needed to make ends meet. I scoured the Help Wanted section of *The New York Times* every morning on the subway coming back from my son's school. I was limited to jobs that allowed me to pick him up in the afternoons. And somewhere and somehow I had to find the time to finish my master's thesis at Hunter and paint.

I found a listing for teaching English to aspiring models. I researched the borough of Queens, where I'd never stepped foot, and figured out a way to trek by subway to the outer reaches, for an interview at a shopping mall. The "school" was two small ramshackle rooms situated on top of an outlet store. The classroom consisted of twelve brown metal folding chairs and two overhead fluorescent light fixtures. I landed the job at fifteen bucks an hour for two hour-and-a-half sessions per week.

Another stroke of good luck from the Help Wanted ads found me two subway stops away teaching journalism at a junior college. Sixteen bucks an hour for the same two days a week.

The roving editor routine plus the two Queens jobs broke me down. I was thrilled to have the work, but soon I felt that I was counting out my life, not in coffee spoons but in endless subway loops. The time spent belowground added up to far more than the time I spent in class.

After a semester of this grind, luck again came my way. A friend told me that Bloomingdale's needed a copywriter. They liked my credentials and hired me for two full days a week, and I could still leave early enough to pick up my son at school.

Around the same time, *The New York Times* posted a listing for a journalism teacher at the Fashion Institute of Technology. After four interviews I acquired a new title, Professor Penney. I told my Queens colleagues that I had found work in the city for the next semester, and the aspiring models air-kissed me good-bye. I was switching employers at a dizzying rate, but I finally began to feel some financial stability and that, at last, my life was definitely on the right track.

CHAPTER 10

The Kindness of
Friends and Strangers

MF + 5 WEEKS

Since the MF, I wake up every morning at 4:46 by the red lights of the digital clock. Anxiety twists through my veins. I imagine that if I curl into the tightest ball maybe I can crush it away. But it's no good, of course. To short-circuit the demons, I snap out of bed, pull open the curtains, gaze out onto a magnificent platinum moon in the luminous gray-blue sky.

The world appears to be exactly the same as it was BMF. Some skyscrapers are already alight with worker bees booting up their computers—or maybe they've been there all night on overtime hours to make ends meet. Suspendered, bespoke, pin-striped-suited, John Lobb–custom-shod bankruptcy lawyers are making big bucks in this economy so they, too, are probably arriving before dawn to strategize their day. More windows are illuminated by early-rise type-A moguls frantically counting the millions they are losing in the meltdown. At first glance, the scene may look as it always has for the last ten years, but inside those offices, everything may actually be very different.

I pad into the kitchen with its gleaming granite counters and its maple and glass cupboards loaded with beautiful china that I've collected over the years. My mother, although withholding in many ways, gave me trays and plates and bowls made of sterling silver from the time I was a young girl. She was certain, I'm sure, that I would lead a life in which these items would be in constant use. Hence I developed an early delight in fine things, and I embarked on the high road to the slow accumulation of Baccarat glasses and exquisite china—all potential items for eBay now. As I wait for the coffee to drip into my mug and peer out the window, I can see the Lipstick Building, as New Yorkers have nicknamed Philip Johnson's rounded, pink edifice. What an irony! From my own window, I can see directly to the MF's offices, where he did his scheming and stealing and where my savings disappeared. As I look at it, I feel the now-familiar gut-sickening rise of panic. What am I going to do? What if I fall ill? What will happen to me? SNT—now!

An adjoining apartment building obstructs a small part of my view but I am always tracking the light in a unit that is a few floors above me. Summer, winter, fall, and spring, a light is always on. I can see the glow at all hours of the night, and during the day if the sun isn't shining. Rays of chilly fluorescence emanate from the window. I imagine they're from an

old staticky television with bent rabbit ears or from an insti-
tutional overhead unit that sheds an unblinking cold light
onto a dreary room with old stained brown Barcaloungers
facing the decades-old television set and tables full of yellow
prescription bottles and greasy bifocals.

The sad light has beamed out of the windows for at least
a dozen years. I've always wondered who lives there. I visualize an old woman who sits in one of those chairs, with a
raggedy crocheted blanket at her feet, unable to read because
her eyes have undiagnosed cataracts or macular degenera-
tion. She is afraid of the dark.

The building is in a good neighborhood and quite fancy,
with its own part-time doorman, so I imagine that she has
enough money to have an aide come in during the day a few
days a week so that she can be found in case she should fall
and break a hip on her way to the bathroom. The aide, an
unsmiling woman, would have her own family in Ecuador
or Colombia and is sending money home to her children; she
makes sure the TV chatters nonstop to give a feeling of life in
the airless room. She cooks some canned soup for her client,
who never complains. But maybe there's no aide at all, and
it's a social worker assigned to the woman's case who stops by
weekly.

This old woman of my imagination is lucky. She has a
roof over her head, enough money to pay the rent, maintain
minimum electricity, and pay the aide, if indeed there is
one. She probably has a telephone to call 911 and of course
she has her television.

When the demons descend on me, the image is starkly

worse and more tormented. I'm alone and abandoned in a state hospital with some sort of slowly suppurating terminal illness, with attendants who don't care about anything except a paycheck to feed their families. I'm just waiting to die and wishing I had had the foresight to get my hands on some capsules of almondy cyanide to wipe me out of the horrible world I've found myself in.

I wonder if my fear of institutions comes from the year my mother spent at the Payne Whitney Psychiatric Clinic after her nervous breakdown when I was six. I heard whispers about "electroshock" and words like "convulsive," but no one would tell me what they meant. I knew they were something scary. From my grandmother's house in Boston, I would talk to my mother every Sunday on a staticky phone with a gummy black receiver by an old brown sofa with lumpy springs. Her voice was always sad and far away. My grandmother had very little time for me, and one of the clearest visions of my childhood is of my aunt's tall green oxygen tanks and nurses caring for the dying woman with scary, blue-blotched skin and small atrophied legs, whose large airless room was next to my small dark one.

....

It's close to six a.m. now and the papers have finally been deposited at my door. I must remember to stop delivery today, as I need to save every dollar and I don't read them anyway. Since the MF terrorized me, it's impossible to read the news because that rictus smile of his is everywhere, with hun-

I'd rather know for sure that I'm not getting the SIPC money than dwell in this excruciating limbo. And why do I need to know the worst-case scenario? Because, says Professor Gilbert, "When we get bad news we weep for a while, and then get busy making the best of it. We change our behavior, we change our attitudes. We raise our consciousness and lower our standards. We find our bootstraps and tug. But we can't come to terms with circumstances whose terms we don't yet know. An uncertain future leaves us stranded in an unhappy present with nothing to do but wait."

....

Thank god it's Monday morning! The light hasn't dawned but I'm at the studio, where I spend the day Photoshopping dozens of photographs from vivid color to mordant black and white, shredding dozens more that aren't quite good enough.

Today I'm contacting the phone, cable, gas, electric, Internet, and paper delivery providers to renegotiate service or to stop them altogether. I lower my cable bill by thirty bucks a month, my phone bill by twenty-two (it's still high but I cannot relinquish access to the outside world), but the rest won't budge. I'll maintain *The New York Times* home delivery for a short while but that will have to join the rest of the heap of "luxuries" that must go. The next hour and a half is spent trading endless phone calls to confer with bankers and lawyers.

When I drag myself through the front door of my apartment that evening, exhausted, a lush spray of fragrant yellow

dreds of inches of print about him dominating the pages. Plus, if I start reading, the unbelievable irresponsibility of the SEC will overwhelm me with anger.

I down my coffee to the dregs, stuff a load of laundry into the washer, and spy the shiny canister of a new rug cleaner stowed under the sink next to the box of Tide.

I get to work scrubbing out every spot—even the pinpoint-size ones—on the carpets in the bedroom and living room. I will have these carpets for the rest of my life. The furniture better be polished and each new crack tended to. No breakdowns or scratches or wine spills allowed. How could I pay for refinishing, reslipcovering?

Everything must last until my last minute on this earth. It's not an upbeat thought. But eradicating the stains is cathartic, and reminds me that I still have some control. It's the loss of control that really is the root of all my panic and wild imaginings. When I had my hard-earned money, starting way back in those years when I was working multiple jobs to support my son, I felt I had some control over what would happen to me. This morning, however, I at least have some control over my rugs.

Saturday and Sunday are mostly spent in more bouts of terror and body-paralyzing panic, with calls and e-mails from Richard and Alex to calm me down. This weekend is a low point—the shock is over, the adrenaline of the first weeks has waned, the noise about my blog has quieted, and I'm alone with my new reality. I am swilling down tranquilizers but at the same time being careful not to take too many. I worry about addiction—another problem that I surely can do without. I need to find a psychopharmacologist who can tell me about the safety of the Klonopin I've been taking, and whether there's anything else that might help with this horrible anxiety.

When I called my internist the morning after the MF catastrophe, I mentioned my dark ideas about hemlock and almondy-smelling capsules.

"Thoughts are not actions," he said. "You haven't done anything to hurt yourself. But there's another way to look at this. Right now you have very little control over what's happening to you. By telling yourself you have an out you are saying you have control over something, your own life. You are actually doing something healthy, exerting control. As long as your thoughts don't translate into actions, you're fine."

I have no control over what happens with the SIPC money, and it torments me. Because I had money in an IRA account, my situation is different from most of the other investors. Each day yields a different response—different and, maybe, worse. I'm often told, "Don't expect a cent." Other lawyers and victims I've met through e-mail say "Maybe $100,000, but don't count on it." On a great day, someone will respond, "It's possible you could recover the full $500,000 from the SIPC." But no one can say anything for sure. There are no rules about who's getting—or not getting—what or when, if ever. It could be a decade or more before the bureaucrats at the SIPC decide what to pay out and to whom.

Everywhere I look I face uncertainty. Before December 11, when I saw the market going haywire and the news-

papers writing about a "deep recession," I believ[e] if I lost a good percentage of my savings, with careful budgeting I would still have enough mon[ey] on, even if I had to make major changes. But to l[ose every] cent? To be robbed? I'd never conceived of robbery [because] they weren't part of my bag lady fears. A reasonable am[ount] of money in my Madoff savings made the terrors lose s[ome] of their potency and I had been pretty sure that, even w[ith] the meltdown, I could survive decently.

Now I live in a claustrophobic shroud of ambiguity. Wil[l] I receive the SIPC insurance proceeds? How much money can I reasonably expect to earn—if any? Will it ever be possible to have a small but reassuring amount of money in the bank, so if another catastrophe occurs I can weather it?

This skyrocketing uncertainty is the most debilitating and disheartening aspect of what I'm now facing and I'm certain it's the cause of my four a.m. anxiety attacks. A psychologist at Harvard, Daniel Gilbert, recently wrote about uncertainty in an op-ed piece in *The New York Times*. He described an experiment involving shocks in which some participants knew in advance they would always get an intense shock, while others knew they would have only a few intense shocks along with a series of milder ones. Those who had been told beforehand they would always receive an intense shock showed fewer symptoms of fear, such as rapid heartbeat or profuse sweating, than those who did not know when the intense shocks were coming. Gilbert wrote, "People feel worse when something bad *might* occur than when something bad *will* occur."

roses greets me. The elegant cellophane wrapping with long, streaming yellow ribbons is unmistakable. They are from Peggy, Zezé, Doris, and Walter, my friends and neighbors at Zezé flowers around the corner. For years, they gave me ravishing and unusual flowers to use in my photographs. Tucked beside the glass vase is a note of love from the gang. When I smell the fragrance of those saffron-colored roses, I think back to the evening of December 11, the last time I bought a bouquet for myself.

The flowers are just the beginning of wonderful gestures from friends and strangers alike. People have read the blogs. They write that they'd had a visceral response to my story. My e-mail overflows with notes of empathy and sympathy and encouragement. The United States mail delivers more letters from friends and people I have never met—from as far away as England, Germany, Sweden, Spain, and Japan. Notes and cards come to the studio from strangers who have somehow managed to track me down even though my name is misspelled in the phone book. If you've had a bad thing happen to you and someone takes the time out from a very busy life to set pen to paper, or to write a thoughtful e-mail, the world seems a more humane, habitable place indeed. I like to think I've done the right thing by friends in need over the years, but now more than ever I know the power of small kindnesses.

Many, many friends have reached out to me in immensely generous ways. Cathryn says she would like to pay the rent on the studio for a month, until I can see my way clear to what my next steps with my work might be.

Stephen, a longtime Condé Nast pal, practically has me belly-laughing the way I did in the old days when he calls and declares, "I know you, girlfriend, you'll want to stay with your fancy colorist, Kyle. An uptown girl like you wants to look her best. And honey, I know these colorists. They are definitely not cheap. You've gotta let me pay! I did it for my aunt, now I want to do it for you!"

"You may be right," I say. "Thank god I had the roots done two days before the MF thing. I *am* nervous about home-colored highlights. I could very easily turn out looking like a Russian hooker a century past her prime—"

"Let me do this for you!" he says. "Call me when you want highlights and a blow-dry!"

My friends Alice and Tommy call almost every day. They invite me to get some sun with them down in the Caribbean, to stay in their weekend house. Tommy asks me: "What is your strategy, AP?"

"Strategy?" I reply in a sort of dazed way. "I haven't thought of a strategy. I'm just panicky and poor."

"I'll sit down with you and go over the numbers," he says. Tommy is a serious money guy and this is an amazing offer. "Let's see how you're going to get through this."

Several weeks later, he huddles with me in a corner of an Italian trattoria, pen and paper in hand. At the end of lunch, I have homework to do: fill numbers into the columns he's made and make careful lists of how much money I spend each month, another list of rock-bottom necessities, and yet another of possible income sources. He is optimistic that we'll find a way to pay the rent for the studio. We'll meet again to detail a new budget. Here is a busy, important guy, a chairman of major boards, taking hours out of his day to help me with basic arithmetic! My world is still shattered into a million shards but my friends are helping me to glue it back together. Good friends, I'm beginning to think, might be the best cure for bag lady syndrome.

Since writing the blogs, I've done several TV and radio shows where I've commented on the MF. A producer at CNN called about a story on the MF and his victims, *Madoff: Secrets of a Scandal*. It turns out that the host of the report, Christine Romans, identifies with my fears of being a bag lady. We discussed how we both have worked and saved and feared that all our hard-earned money would disappear and we'd end up homeless and frightened and alone.

I agreed to be on the show, if they would come to the studio. I can do it only between the calls I have to make to the lawyers and accountant who are helping me with Madoff-related work, such as filing the SIPC insurance claim. All the MF's casualties must hire professionals to decipher the arcane language of the endless forms. Another outrage that assails me almost daily.

The CNN program spawned something like two million Web site click-throughs on my "victim" story (I prefer the word "casualty" because it implies wounds that all of us have sustained). One minute after the program aired on a Saturday night I received two messages on my answering machine. The first was a lawyer from New Jersey, phoning with his wife to say how sorry they were about my recent and ongoing travails. They said that I had real courage and felt sure I'd be okay. A few days later, I called the number they left to thank them for their concern and their encouraging words.

A woman from New Canaan left a message at my studio: "I've never done anything like this before," she said, "and please don't think I'm crazy but you sound like a sincere person who is really in trouble. I'm divorced and live in New Canaan, Connecticut, and have a beautiful house here. My daughter is getting married soon and if you need a place to stay, you are always welcome here. I mean it."

I phoned Susan—that's her name—and thanked her for the unbelievably generous offer, and tell her I am familiar with how lovely New Canaan is: my parents had lived for more than thirty years in nearby Darien.

"You came across as a genuine person," she said, "and I thought if there is any way I could help. And then I realized I have this big house—"

"You are beyond kind," I said, "but I think I'll be okay. I can stay in my apartment for a while at least, and I'll figure out a way to make money."

"If you ever need time off, a weekend, a month, a year, you would have a space all to yourself. I mean it," she said. I am certain she did.

A few days after my conversation with Susan, I received an e-mail saying, "You have been selected to apply for a grant from the New York Foundation for the Arts." Astonished by the note, I immediately called to find out details but was politely told to fill out the forms and that my application would be reviewed. I did as requested, and just a few days after my call I was approved for a grant. I did my investigative best to find out who was behind this incredible generosity, but the courteous young woman at the Foundation said firmly that the donor "wished to remain anonymous." The person who instigated the grant knows that art is my primary passion and I am indescribably grateful to you, whoever you are. You have helped me in the deepest way possible.

And despite the bad rap lawyers get in my town for being overpriced and overblown, a few of them—strangers before my MF experience—have been unstinting with their time and advice. When you get in a big complicated mess like the one I'm in, you realize why they get paid the big bucks. Brad Friedman, a lawyer at Milberg, was on the MF's case early on. I sat behind him in court the day after the MF was arrested and we waited and waited and waited in vain for him to appear. Brad came to my house for coffee one morning, and although I didn't sign up for a class action suit, he gets back to me instantly on his BlackBerry any time I have a legal question. He really is a decent man and sympathetic to the wreckage that Madoff has wrought. Then, when a friend suggested I get in touch with the hotshot litigator Steve Molo, I e-mailed him about my plight and he called me fifteen minutes later. Lawyers from high-priced white-shoe firms to one-person operatives who just want to help and offer counsel have been in touch with the MF's casualties across the country.

When I get home from the studio on Monday, a blue Brooks Brothers box is waiting for me at home. I haven't ordered anything, of course. One of my favorite activities—

shopping—is out of the question, maybe for the rest of my life.

I have no taste for it. Not a nano-smidgen of desire. Nada. Not only do I have no money, there is nothing in the world I need or want except peace of mind, something that no amount of money can buy. Or can it?

I'm gladly diverted from my thoughts by the Brooks Brothers box. I'm sure there's been a mistake but after I inspect the label and see that it is addressed to me, I open it. Inside a small white envelope lies on a pristine white shirt.

"This is one of my favorite things," writes Nan, a special friend, "and you'll never have to iron it." It's a perfect fit. Who has friends such as these? How lucky can I be!

CHAPTER 11

Everyone Has a Story to Tell

On a cold Christmas morning in the late seventies, when my son was in Vermont with his father, I woke up at about seven o'clock with the sun just blinking into a pale gray-blue sky filled with a few dark clouds scudding behind the industrial buildings of what was now called SoHo. I looked from my second-story window onto my frosted cobblestoned street of West Broadway and saw four black-and-white NYPD squad cars lined up in a row. Two were facing downtown, two were facing uptown, and the cops were talking with one another through open windows. "Feliz Navidad" was blaring on their radios.

I grabbed the bottle of champagne that I kept in my fridge to celebrate good times, flew down to the street in my flannel nightgown and slippers, and handed over the bottle.

"Merry Christmas, officers!" I said. "This is to thank you for being the best cops in the world!" I ran upstairs again, listening to all four sirens punctuate the end of each stanza of "Feliz Navidad" as the cops waved good-bye to me and drove off.

This would have never happened uptown. I felt happy that I lived in this friendly neighborhood and that I had changed my life. But there were many difficult moments when my son was away on weekends or spending time with his dad. The cops; firemen; Mr. Dappolito, the baker around the corner; and Harry, the paint store owner, all were terrific neighbors to us, but when I wasn't working and my friends were busy, I often felt lonely and down.

....

I had met several artists at Hunter who lived downtown or in Brooklyn and we exchanged studio visits and sometimes joined up for pizza and a glass of wine, but I saw very little of my old uptown friends, as any hours not spent with my son were taken up by painting, work-for-money, and school. I went on a few dates over those six years that I lived on West Broadway, and often wished I had more. Here and there a friend would set me up or I'd go to a party hoping to meet a smart, funny, kind guy who was involved in some way with the arts, but I never found anyone who seemed right for me.

My social life was not entirely bleak, however. On summer nights when my son was away for a month at summer camp, some girlfriends and I would shoot uptown to Studio 54, which was in its heyday.

Studio 54 was like an enveloping hallucinogenic drug that could, if you were an addictive type, become central to your existence. The blinding strobe lights razoring through the crowd, the roaring sound of Gloria Gaynor's "I Will Survive" crashing straight into you, the writhing sweaty gorgeous naked torsos of beautiful men who were smashed on sex and music and poppers, gave you an incredible contact high. The sensory experience was so extreme that your mind was neutered and your pure physical body took its place. I would sometimes smoke a joint that a friend had stashed in a pocket or purse but no one ever offered me cocaine. A night at Studio with a group of friends was wild and uninhibited fun, and who doesn't desire that once in a while?

The roving editor job at *Vogue* ended after two years, and the FIT appointment was only for two semesters. I continued to churn out copy for Bloomingdale's and to write freelance articles, but I wanted to be earning enough to put some money away for the proverbial rainy day. Back I went to *The New York Times* Help Wanted listings. I found an opening for a professional writer who would work with retired teachers from union DC 37. I interviewed for the vacancy and landed the job. Two mornings a week I met with a group of men and women who had been public school teachers for most of their lives. Their union provided classes to update their skills in a variety of areas, and writing was one of them. At the beginning of the course, I asked them if they would be willing to keep diaries of their present lives and also to recount how their past affected what they were thinking and doing now.

"Our lives are not very interesting. We're just ordinary people," they protested.

"I'm no good," someone else blurted out. "I can't write a word. Who would care about what I write, even if I could write?"

I worked to set them straight. Everyone has a tale to tell. These people had given so much to the community as teachers, and their stories mattered. I encouraged them to write about their children, their neighbors, their former students, anything at all, but just to write. I remember loosely quoting Hemingway: "If you don't know what to say when you're facing a blank piece of white paper, just put down one sentence of truth. Write 'the sky is blue' or 'my desk is cluttered' and you have a beginning."

After more cajoling, they agreed to write a few pages for the next class.

When the class convened again, I coaxed and convinced each of them to read aloud what they had written—one woman had to do it in Spanish because she was too embarrassed reading in English. Even though most of the students didn't understand Spanish, they all applauded heartily.

Looking back on it, the DC 37 class was one of most important experiences of my career. To watch people who, despite years of service to their community, believe they have nothing to offer the world become excited by their own creative work was a great thrill. Not only that, the enthusiasm of the group was infectious. I had been grappling with my own doubts about whether I was any good as an artist and, at night, fueled by my students' energy, after my son was asleep, instead of passing out with fatigue, I worked furiously on my painting. I'd finally finish cleaning my brushes around two a.m., tired but satisfied that I was making progress. I'd wake up at six to escort my son to school on the subway. Those were the days when I could subsist on four to six hours of sleep a night.

....

A few weeks after the DC 37 class wrapped up, I was working on a Bloomingdale's assignment when my phone rang. It was one of fashion's fabulous women: Carrie Donovan. Carrie was so irate that she didn't get Diana Vreeland's job as editor in chief that she vamoosed from *Vogue* and set up a competitive domain at *The New York Times Magazine*.

"You're such a breezy writer, Alex," Carrie cooed into my ear. "We need you over here at this stuffy place. You'll be a breath of fresh air." This was Carrie-speak for "I need something from you right away."

"Of course," I replied. "What can I do for you?"

"You can be here at two and we'll have a nice chat," she said as if she were certain I didn't have another plan in sight for the next decade. I could reach Forty-third Street by two, and still make it to school to pick up my son, so again I said "Of course." My assignment was to write an article every other week for *The New York Times Magazine* in the fields of art, lifestyle, fitness, and beauty, or whatever Carrie Donovan deemed might "amuse" the readers. I accepted the job.

Carrie Donovan, a midwesterner at heart and by birth, was famous for her gargantuan horn-rim glasses, which reached from the tops of her eyebrows to the bottoms of her cheeks. She never ventured out into the world during working hours—which to her encompassed all hours of the day and night—without her two strands of creamy white, fake, bosom-level Kenneth Jay Lane pearls. Almost six feet tall, square-faced and waistless, she wore low-cut clothes to accentuate the pearls or the boobs, though we could never figure out which were most important to her. Some called her a *jolie laide,* others said she just wanted to get laid. She was handsome in a theatrical, drag-queen kind of way and commanded total attention whenever she was in the room.

One day I walked into her office and she was wearing a foot-high paisley-printed emerald-green turban. Hanging from the folds of fabric was a huge rhinestone-encrusted pin that just scraped the horn-rims. The rest of the outfit consisted of a revealing white ruffled peasant blouse, the two strands of pearls, of course, and an orange printed peasant skirt that twinkled with sequins and swirled to her ankles. On her feet were crimson espadrilles. Each element was a bit bizarre but she put them all together in her Carrie Donovan way, carrying off the look with nonchalance and in-the-know authority.

As we were sitting there, her phone rang and it was Abe Rosenthal, who was the managing editor of the paper at the time and who scared the bejeezus out of all the staff—except Carrie. She'd tell us, "He's such an adorable man. You just need to flirt with him a bit."

Abe Rosenthal adorable? Someone to flirt with? Whirling skirts and espadrilles at the newspaper of record, the stately *New York Times*? The whole routine boggled us. But she was enthusiastic in the extreme about each of our assignments no matter how pokey or prosaic, and she inspired real excellence in a way that Miss G from my old *Vogue* days could never have done.

"Abe needs me," she said, rising dramatically from the little gold bamboo chair that she sat in when working at her table. As she swirled the peasant skirt I could see not one but two crinolines edged with lace, which no doubt gave this unusual article of office attire an amazing buoyancy.

Before she descended to the third floor where Abe awaited her, she opened a small drawer on the antique tabouret by her table (I'll never know how she convinced the *Times* to give her a table; most of the editors there toiled at big gray metal desks) and withdrew a perfume bottle, the kind that my mother used to keep on her dressing table. Attached to the bottle—French crystal I'm sure—was a small net-covered bulb on a very fine net-covered tube. She pinched the bulb and a heavy mist of Calvin Klein perfume dissolved into the air. She squeezed the thing a couple more times, replaced it in the drawer, and flounced down the hall, leaving vast vapor trails of fragrance among those of us who slogged through our copy in the anonymous cubicles outside of her office. My life then seemed to be made up of extremes— from uptown leafy green Park Avenue to downtown grease-slicked cobblestone streets, from Smith College to Rosedale Fish Market, from the rarified airs of Carrie Donovan and

The New York Times to the grungy room where I taught retired New York City public school teachers—but I thrived
on those dichotomies.

I worked like a dog on my first story, which was on the
new wave of hairdressers who were opening ateliers around
town. I wrote and rewrote it. And rewrote it again. Finally, I
thought it had the gloss that Carrie wanted and the gravitas—
if there were a way to instill that into an article about
hairstylists—that the *Times* was known for. I placed the copy
in the in-box on her assistant's desk and hoped for the best.

An hour later, Carrie warbled into the phone: "Alex,
dear one, would you be kind enough to come into my office?

"Your piece is wonderful, just marvelous," she trilled,
looking at me through the top of her huge horn-rims. "I'm
turning it over to the Copy department so they can put it
into English."

I was horrified and completely humiliated. I knew I
should never have tried to write anything beyond copy.
Who did I think I was, believing I could do a piece that
would appear in *The New York Times*?

Little did I know this was standard operating procedure
for Ms. Donovan. She trusted other editors to give any story
a *Times* veneer and, indeed, what I had thought was good
was much better when the copy people finished with it.

When I returned to my cubicle, my direct editor came in
and sat down in the single straight-back aluminum chair allotted to each of us.

"Do you have your first draft of this?" she asked. I pulled

out the first of my dozen-plus tries and gave it to her. I thought she would take it with her but she sat right there and read it word for word while I waited with anxiety accelerating by the second. I was certain she was about to fire me on the spot.

"From now on, just give Carrie your first draft. What you've done here is fine. I'd change only a few phrases. Trust me on this."

I decided to have faith in what she was telling me: after all she'd been at the *Times* for many years. I cut down my drafts from ten to three or four. After that first calamity, all was pretty much smooth sailing and I ended up actually enjoying working at the magazine, although I never, for even one moment, relished writing.

My stories at the *Times* caught the attention of a colleague from my *Glamour* days, Phyllis Starr Wilson, the then executive editor. She had presented the Boss of Bosses with a new concept for a magazine called *Self.* It would be a monthly publication for smart women who wanted to stay healthy, intellectually, physically, and emotionally. He liked her idea and *Self* was the first magazine Condé Nast had launched in decades. The idea of a publication named *Self,* which was not about selfishness, but about the awareness and power of one's self, was new, and the magazine became a success in a very short time. *Self* was eventually to play a very significant role in my life.

Phyllis commissioned me to do several stories, and one day, while I was at my desk at the *Times,* she phoned and said urgently, "We're practically at release time. My lead cover story just fell through. Do you have any ideas you can work on right now?"

My mind whipped into Condé Nast emergency-room mode. I thought for half a second and rattled off a couple notions that might do the trick. "Mmm, not quite right for the cover, but good for inside stories," she said.

"Oh, wait a minute," I said. "What about 'how to make love to a man'?"

I'd finally met a man on a blind date who met my requirements of smart and funny and kind and involved in the arts. Chris was a visually oriented geologist who lived in New Mexico, where he taught and did arcane research. At the time, a long-distance relationship seemed a good idea to me as I had too much on my plate to consider anything more permanent.

We'd just spent a lovely weekend together when Chris had said to me—in the kindest, gentlest way anyone could—"You really need to know more about what a man wants in bed."

I was shocked—and embarrassed. I thought I was pretty sophisticated and quite adept in the erotic arena but it seemed that I didn't have a clue.

He had been so tender and sweet that I responded, "Well, can you teach me?"

During his next visits, I had quite a few intriguing lessons. Sadly, the long-distance situation, as is so often the case, did not work out and we parted ways a few months later. I missed our daily phone calls and wished I could meet another man with whom I could fall in love, but I certainly never forgot those tutorials.

"Perfect! Sounds great!" Phyllis said after I threw out the idea. "When can you deliver? I need about two thousand words a week from Friday."

"I can do it pretty fast," I assured her, knowing that any stop-the-press deadline is padded with several days to spare for rewrites and gathering illustrations. "But I'm not sure about next Friday; can you give me till tomorrow to think it through? I have a *Times* piece due in two days."

"Okay," she agreed.

I interrupted her before she could say more, knowing she would push me to do the work she wanted.

"And line up something else in case I can't do it. I don't want to leave you without something to print."

She laughed and said, "All right, but it's a fantastic idea and I really want it!"

Phyllis Wilson never minced words. If she didn't like a story idea you knew it straightaway. And she didn't like many stories that she herself hadn't thought of. So I knew it would make a good article, but did I have the time to write it?

My son was spending that evening at his father's, and I thought a great deal about the idea that had rolled off my tongue so easily.

I phoned Phyllis the next day and said I couldn't do the story. I needed more time to think about how to approach it. Some gut instinct told me if I didn't know what a man wanted in bed, there were thousands of other women who didn't know either. My idea could develop into a book—and if it was a book, I could make more money than just writing an article.

I knew I was putting Phyllis in a bind but nonetheless

told her I wanted to give the story a try as a book proposal and assured her I'd write a couple of articles for her in the next several months.

"I want your word of honor that *Self* gets first-serial rights," she said. I remember smiling about the notion of actually writing a book and seeing it excerpted in *Self* magazine as we hung up.

CHAPTER 12

If You Think You Have No Options, Think Again

Several people have commented on how ascetically and minimally I lived during the decade I spent downtown. My parents, who still had their house in Darien, Connecticut, deigned to trek to the wilds of SoHo only once. My relationship with them, strained due to their formality and extreme strictness during my teenage and college years, fractured after they refused to attend my wedding for reasons that were never clear to me until many years later when I saw Dr. J, the psychiatrist who played a crucial role in my life. They continued to score low on the essential parental traits of nurturing, but they were caring and loving grandparents and adored their grandchild, wanting to spend as much time as they could with him. My son and I would take the train to Connecticut every few weeks so they could all be together and enjoy gardening and cooking and museum and zoo-going, activities they'd carefully and thoughtfully planned for his hours there.

On a cool but sunny Saturday in the spring, my parents climbed the flight of steps to my little loft apartment while Pookabee furiously wagged her tail to welcome them. A few hours before their arrival, wanting to show off our little place, I'd biked up to the flower market on Twenty-sixth Street and bought several bunches of sumptuous parrot tulips and arranged them in the silver vases that my mother had given me. I thought the colorful floral counterpoints made the simple room look stylish and contemporary.

After a few minutes of hugging and kissing their wonderful grandchild, my father, who rarely had much to say, asked, "Where is the furniture?" and then added, "I'm surprised I haven't seen any rats."

Rats? I shuddered and began to feel the same kind of anger that had flooded me at their inexplicable aversion to my ex-husband. I chose to laugh off his comments. I had long ago stopped confronting my parents when they made nasty or inflammatory remarks.

I was a fastidious housekeeper and I had made sure our space was airtight—no rodents of any sort could have intruded—but my father was right that there wasn't much furniture. I hadn't had time for decoration even though my environment has always been of primary importance to me. I try to make my surroundings simple and tasteful and convey a sense of ease and tranquillity. I'm visually oriented and if I walk into a cluttered or badly designed room, I'm uncomfortable and have a great urge to flee. My decor aesthetics—then and now—were minimalist not only because of budget constraints but because I felt physically more at ease and relaxed without knickknacks and useless objects on tables and walls. I didn't hang my own paintings—and still do not hang my photographs—as I thought it too self-referential to say nothing of self-reverential. To this day I prefer my walls to be bare so I can imagine what beautiful paintings or photographs or drawings might belong there. If a home is "perfect" or "finished" it is, for me, a moribund space. There's no leeway for the exciting possibilities of change or growth.

As long as my son was happy in his room, which was crammed with fire engines and model airplanes and Matchbox cars and two-way-radio parts and shelves loaded down with books and souvenirs, I was happy about what I thought of as my own strict Bauhaus surroundings in the rest of our living quarters.

After a year of living in SoHo, two trestle tables and four folding chairs were the only furniture that adorned the small downstairs space. I used them as dining tables and work tables when I was painting or writing. Upstairs was my son's personal domain, with a small alcove that housed a bed and a minuscule closet for me. I didn't need much room for clothes as my usual garb consisted of painting jeans worn with old white shirts, blouses, and jackets purchased at my most favorite store, which happened to be downstairs in my own building. Harriet Love, the eponymous shop owner and my private fashion consultant, was a pioneer in the vintage clothing craze and became a close friend. On some Saturdays when my son was away, if she needed an extra salesperson to handle the growing traffic, I'd traipse downstairs and pitch in to help with the customers. I loved playing around with the mélange of clothes and accessories that she brought in almost daily.

If I wrote *How to Make Love to a Man* as a book, I reasoned that the extra money would be well spent in making our space a bit homier and both my son and I could finally invite friends to come over. I would have racks built for canvases, and shelves made to hold my painting supplies. I would splurge on an old and gnarled refectory table I'd seen at an antique shop on Thirteenth Street, some interesting chairs to go with it, a sofa—if one could fit into the small room—a couple of good pots so I could begin to cook more seriously again. I might even have enough to buy something to rest my upstairs mattress on. I estimated it would take about seven thousand dollars to give our little place some much-needed stylistic improvements.

I spent a few days writing up the book proposal, then realized I'd need a book agent to sell it. Who do you go to when you need literary advice? Your hairdresser, who else?

My Japanese stylist, Suga, had a high fashion-magazine profile. I knew him from several *Vogue* shoots and we'd become pals. One evening, when the salon had just closed, we chatted over small glass cups of chilled sake and agreed to trade skills. I would try to teach him enough English so he could more easily communicate his sharp wit and humor.

He, in turn, would cut my hair. I clearly had the best of the bargain. During the months that I was his English tutor I also helped him write a book that was published for the opening of his Fifty-seventh Street salon. I figured he could recommend me to his book agent.

Suga was, as I said, a big deal in hairdressing and he was also much in demand for important fashion shoots. He told me a story once while cutting my hair that I've never forgotten, as it taught me a valuable lesson for both my professional and personal life.

Vogue had flown Suga to Egypt for a shoot at the top of the pyramids. As the crew was climbing to their destination, the editor had a "eureka" moment.

"The look I see here now," she said, shading her eyes with her hand and peering out on the vastness of the desert broken only by the geometry of the ancient pyramids, "the look must be soft, waving hair streaming into the golden light of the morning."

During the weeks of planning that went into the shoot, the editor had requested stick-straight hair with right-angled bangs. Accordingly, Suga had been up half the night achieving the requisite glossy and vertical style.

Suga, now on top of a pyramid with a command to create waving curls, was a veteran of many exotic and expensive shoots, and he understood well that there are no such words as "No, I don't think we can do that right now." This unflappability was one of the things that made him so invaluable in a tight situation and why he was paid the Very Big Bucks.

To be successful on a magazine shoot, you must possess the ability to prepare for any occurrence that should never happen—but sometimes does. Standing under the cool cobalt sky that lay behind the pyramids, he remembered a tiny pink-colored clay Egyptian oil-burning lamp he'd picked up at a local bazaar and tucked into his chic backpack.

Suga's custom-fitted Goyard case always held a curling iron, and on this trip he had enough styling oil to dress a hundred salads. He had reckoned that it would slick down the models' hair should there be a frizz-making drop of humidity in the desert. He now carefully poured the fluid into the spout of the oil lamp, which, most luckily, had the remains of an old wick inside it, and proceeded to heat the curling iron over the small flame that the lamp had produced.

"What if there hadn't been a wick? What if there hadn't been an oil lamp?" I asked.

"Something would have come to me, it *had* to," he said, with a very slight smile. "I would have lit anything I could to make that curling iron work!"

The moral of Suga's story that endures with me today is: even if you think you have no options, think again. Unless you've been mummified you have choices and alternatives.

When my mind goes into a gridlock of anxiety, as it has done with great frequency lately, reason deserts me. Everything coagulates and my brain is deadlocked. I can't make a decision; alternatives and options elude me. Sometimes the one thing that can jolt me into action is to remember Suga straddling a magnificent pyramid, heating a small black-handled curling iron with an ancient pinkish-hued oil lamp.

....

Well, there I was, relaxing in Suga's salon chair with a delicate porcelain cup of steaming green tea, as he precisely clipped my hair lock by lock. I asked him about his book agent, and he wrote down her name and number with a calligraphic pen in his elegant script. I sent the agent, Connie Clausen, my book proposal the next morning.

Two days later she called me and, without a preamble, said that she believed she could get "good money" for my idea. I was thrilled. I let myself dream that it could be as much as ten thousand dollars! She had already contacted several houses that were interested and she wanted to take me for an interview at the one she thought would best publish the book.

Dressed in the most conservative clothing I owned from my long-ago *Glamour* days, a gray Ralph Lauren pantsuit and my only well-worn pair of Manolos, I met Connie, clad entirely in shades of pink, at 2 Park Avenue, the offices of Clarkson Potter, then owned by a grizzled and aged eminence named Nat Wartels.

Mr. Wartels sat in an enormous office behind a stupendous mahogany desk piled high with manuscripts and yellowing copies of *The New York Times*. At least a half dozen ashtrays were filled with mashed cigar and cigarette butts.

He and his team discussed my idea among themselves,

asked me a few questions, and then the portly Mr. Wartels rose up, walked over to my chair, placed his hand on the back of it, leaned down over me with fetid breath, and asked, "How do you think you'll be able to handle appearing on television?"

"Television?" I repeated. Television? I hadn't thought about going on television. My parents would not like it. I would be fired from the *Times* for writing this kind of book, and I needed the job.

"I was planning on writing under a pseudonym," I said.

He returned to his desk and waved us out of his office.

On the street, I told Connie that there was absolutely and positively no way I could write a sex book under my own name. No way on god's little green earth.

Two hours later Connie called me at home.

"Wartels has offered you a truly enormous advance of seventy-five thousand dollars for *How to Make Love to a Man*—" she said.

"Unbelievable!" I interrupted.

"But," she continued, "you must write it under your own name. You have a classy job and a classy background. They think it is essential for that to come out so the book will have authority and will sell."

"I just can't do it," I said. "I just can't. I have a son to think about. I have parents who would freak out."

We hung up, but not before she convinced me to sleep on it. Oh my good god in heaven!!!! I could not even conceive of what I would do with seventy-five thousand dollars—minus, of course, the agent's ten percent fee. I could quit all my jobs and paint. Perhaps I could get a gallery show. Anything seemed possible!

But alas, I thought before falling asleep, I couldn't compromise my name, or embarrass my son, or lose my other jobs by writing a sex book. Even for that kind of money.

CHAPTER 13

My New Life as a Person of Reduced Circumstances (PoRC)

It's now deep into January. New York has had a tough winter. Many times this year, our streets have been blanketed with unblemished white snow, which is quickly converted into piles of gray-black slush streaked with yellow dog urine. The bone-biting cold is relentless. The MF was arrested a little over a month ago. I spend most of my nights at home, collapsed from working like a lunatic at the studio and dealing with landlords, lawyers, and tax consequences.

The *Times* is being delivered for one more week, but I haven't looked at a paper since the day Madoff confessed to his crimes. I don't want to know what's going on in the world right now. It's as if I've been in a car crash and I haven't emerged from the wreckage yet. I think of those elderly widows whose husbands left their money in the MF's hands trusting that he would "take care" of their wives. These are women who have no resources now. Some will be lucky enough to live with their children. What will happen to the others?

Tonight I am thinking of all the lives that have been ruined by this man. I'm watching reports on TV about how Madoff got away with his crimes. The SEC, supposedly the protection for investors like me, has been negligent and derelict, to say the least. Over and over red flags were raised, warning that the MF's operation was unlawful. Thank god the new Congress thinks the SEC is as despicable as I do.

Hiding behind SEC-speak for "I plead the Fifth," the director of the division of enforcement, Linda Thomsen, said "I can't comment" with a weird crooked-mouth grin when questioned yesterday. Not only are the so-called regulators hiding behind the apron strings of Baby Dubya, who appointed them, they are also showing their true dereliction of duty and humanity. They just want to save their own well-padded civil-servant butts. But it's not just them; the whole system seems to be rigged. It was actually said at the congressional hearings yesterday that the SEC is there to *protect business from the investors* and that the Financial Industry Regulatory Authority (FINRA) *is in bed with industry and corrupt.*

....

If I spend too much time thinking about the MF I don't function very well. Much better to dwell on my new life, which is once again full of dichotomies. Two nights ago, I was sipping Cristal—probably $200 a bottle—from an antique flute glass and having a marvelous dinner with Richard, who, with Alex, helped me with my first blog in what seems like an age ago.

It was one of those mean, polar New York nights and Richard and his charming wife, Jennifer, were entertaining a business friend from London who happened to be wearing an old navy-blue Hermès jacket, a bit tattered but still in good shape.

"It's very old and very warm and comforting," he said, when one of us commented that he didn't have a heavy coat on. "I use Magic Marker when the edges start to shred," he explained, displaying his cuffs, which each of us inspected closely. No trace of his penmanship was to be found—a very handy tip for future use.

Richard cracked open the champagne (sent to him by an advertiser in the Old Days of Excess, barely a few months ago) because he'd heard I'd landed a book deal. You can't live a nightmare every minute. The advance allows me to keep the studio going for a few more months and gives me some breathing room until I'm able to sell whatever I can to start a quail-size nest egg again.

Now here's the dichotomy: two nights ago, I was swizzling expensive champagne, the kind I liked to stash in my own fridge, and this morning I bought a $20 MetroCard and then, instead of tossing the old one, by mistake threw the new one into a trash can on the platform. It was too tall to reach into and I immediately wanted to turn it upside down and dump the contents to find my card. Of course, it would be like looking for a Burmese ruby on the back of a garbage truck. I realized I was freaking out and finally boarded a train. But I couldn't ditch the loss of the card for a couple of hours.

Loss, defeat, and weariness haunt me. Bag ladies have lost everything. At least that is how I see them, trudging their way alone through the streets, with rheumy eyes and frozen hands. I am only a PoRC and a supremely lucky one to have my health and to be escaping the recent single-digit temperatures and heading down south again next week. Another pal, who travels by private jet, offered me a lift. Yes, a PJ. No matter how high I am flying, I am quickly brought down to earth trying to figure out if there is public transportation to the airport in Teterboro, New Jersey, because cab fare and car service are definitely not in my budget.

Even though people are fully aware that jets are polluting the atmosphere and helping to destroy the planet, flying in your own PJ is still considered one of the ultimate perks of having money—and it brings up a provocative question: Is it worse to have had money and lost it? Or is it worse never to have had money at all? I'm not sure I know the answer yet.

....

I'm still waiting to negotiate the rent on my studio with my landlord. He keeps canceling appointments, not a good sign. I send him frantic e-mails every day or so, saying I need to talk to him. I pulled out some old flower prints, thinking it will seem like spring on my studio walls and it may tempt him to barter a bit as my inflatable girls will definitely not ring his bell.

One of my new heroes, a thoughtful public servant, Representative Gary Ackerman (D-NY), pointedly addressed the tight-lipped SEC and FINRA people yesterday saying, "We thought the enemy was Madoff. It was you."

And, to add more insult to the injuries of those who have been Madoff'd, the massive list of the MF's casualties, 13,567 names long (so far), was released yesterday with their home addresses. How many crooks have more than thirteen thousand victims? Those are the kinds of numbers allotted to an evil fiend who commits war crimes.

The MF continues to rollick in his glam penthouse. He knew the system, gamed the system—and he's still gaming it! I visualize him snug and warm on this frigid fourteen-degree day in his silk-lined cashmere robe, illegal Cuban Cohibas in hand, chuckling about the SEC/FINRA hearings on C-SPAN, daintily picking at his chocolate-filled brioche, reaching for his steaming latte and freshly squeezed OJ on a silver tray, and using his phone to move his money right under the noses of his security guards, paid for by his poor "victim" wife, Ruthie— with whose money exactly? The other victims', of course!

So, while the MF is probably sipping Dom to congratulate himself once again for staying out of jail, I am treating myself to a night out and am heading for a friend's birthday party, via a taxi no less—the PoRC's version of a PJ.

My good friend Sarah's husband throws a birthday bash for her every year. Usually it's at a stylish and out-of-the-way restaurant that has yet to be discovered. But this year no one really feels like celebrating. A friend's annual Chinese New Year's fete has been canceled, book parties are rare, charity events are suffering, so Sarah's husband has pared down the guest list and is opting for an evening buffet dinner at their elegant Park Avenue apartment.

When I arrive, Sarah gives me a special hug as she asks how I am and walks me into the living room, which is filled with many people I know. I have no problem joining a group discussing the emptiness of trendy joints around town and how pleasurable it is to be in someone's home.

I leave them in order to nab a smoked salmon hors d'oeuvre in the dining room. An odd feeling comes over me. Guests are poking around the table and chatting, but as soon as I enter, people seem to scatter into other rooms. This is not at all like the party I went to in Florida as a PoRC. I have the distinctly uncomfortable feeling that people are steering clear of me. I wander back to the living room and an old acquaintance comes up to me saying, "I'm not going to ask how you are. I know how you are!"

"Aah," I say and I can feel the mystery clearing up, "I am really okay. I guess people are thinking I'll be a wreck who can't stop crying or get out of bed." Or, I add to myself, they'll think I'm going ask them for a loan.

She nods sympathetically. "I'm glad to see you're here."

"Of course I'm here!" I respond. "Why wouldn't I be? I've had a shitty experience but that doesn't mean I'm a different person! What am I going do? Weep and wail and moan away my life! I'm not going to be in mourning for money!"

She gives me a big hug, saying, "Well, we didn't know what to expect! I've read your blogs and know you're going through a hard time. . . ."

"True," I respond, "but it doesn't mean I'm not the same person! Now, please, let's forget about me, and tell me what's going on in *your* life!"

I learned something important at Sarah's party. People do feel sorry for you. They do pity you. They don't know what to say to you. They expect that you'll be different somehow. It is like a death and you're treated with great fragility—and, often, you're held at a distance. But unlike a death, you can do something about your losses. You can get right back to work. And waste no time about it! Which is exactly what I'm doing most minutes of each day. And, oh god, I still haven't heard from the damned landlord!

At home, before I turn out the light, I think about my experience at Sarah's. Some people will be uneasy or uncomfortable when they see you because they think you're down and out. Maybe some people who have lost their fortunes give off those vibes. But are you defined by your losses? No! Emphatically underlined, italicized, bold-faced **_NO!!!_**

I can't fall asleep so I turn the light back on and jot down a list of the best ways I've learned—so far—to face adversity:

Stay active; get back to work.

Discipline self not to think about future (very difficult).

Discipline self to SNT (stop negative thinking—also very difficult).

Corollary: recognize and enjoy each good experience (no matter how big or small) to the fullest as it occurs.

Don't eat too much; doesn't feel good to be fat
and poor.

Make list of good things that came out of bad
experience.

Allow self-pity for limited time each day (three
minutes at most).

Suck it up—it could be worse.

....

Losing my savings is, without doubt, the most major setback I've experienced in my life. I was traumatized when I received those phone calls telling me that Bernard Madoff had been arrested and that everything I'd ever earned and saved was gone. I still wake up with hideous anxiety racing through my veins and making my heart pound at 4:16 in the morning (lately the demons have decided to attack half an hour earlier). But I refuse to be defeated by such an obstacle. I feel surer of this than ever.

There is no way that all of us aren't facing setbacks in this new economic environment. A vast number of Americans have lost incalculable amounts of money. I was certainly keenly aware of those huge losses due to economic forces but I was living in my own personal intensive care unit, a trauma victim who had every cent of my savings and retirement money stolen. But what am I going to do? Hide under the bedcovers and feel sorry for myself? "Poor little me" is a pathetic, feeble stance. Who wants to spend their time being pathetic? It gets you nowhere. It's okay to feel sorry for yourself every once in a while—and I did. It's human. But for only so long. And then, for me, it's back to work, just as it's been my entire life. What happens if I get sick and can no longer work? I had thought about "retirement" and had saved money that would help me through. And it would have, if I hadn't given it to a crook. But now I'm finding the discipline not to think about anything except what's in front of my nose and, possibly, what's for dinner tonight. While I'm still kicking, I do have hope—or I could drop dead this afternoon. I can't stop to think about it right now. I've got to get on the subway and downtown to work.

CHAPTER 14

How to Make Love to a Man

The evening after my meeting with Nat Wartels, the publisher who wanted to buy my book, I invited a couple of friends over for pizza, and we debated my dilemma.

"I think you should do it," Margo said emphatically. "Everything you do you've done with integrity and a lot of research and serious thought. Even the fish market."

"No, no," I protested. "What would people think? No one would take me seriously again. I don't want people to snicker behind my back, 'Oh, her. She's the one who writes those dirty sex books.'"

"You have to think of how you would write the book," Margo continued. "You're a serious journalist. Would you be reporting? Would it be journalistic?"

"Yes, I wrote in the outline that I wanted to interview men to find out what they needed from women physically and emotionally."

"You're not writing about your own sex life, right?"

"God no, no, no!"

"What's wrong with reporting about an area that interests us all—a lot!"

"I'll lose all my jobs," I said. "No one would ever hire me again."

"If you write this book you won't have time for your other jobs. And when it's over, who knows what might happen."

By the end of the night, the girls had convinced me that if I wrote an honest book as a thoughtful journalist, I would not only stash some money in the bank, I'd be helping women to have better love lives, and, most important, I could afford to rent a real studio and do more of the work I really wanted to do, which was, of course, painting.

I knew painting wasn't a money-making career. If your work sold you were one of the lucky ones. If you could actually live on the money you made, you were blessed. All the painters I knew at the time relied on teaching, waitressing, bartending, or menial jobs to pay the bills. Fortunately, I had freelance writing to fall back on. Failing that, I figured I could probably nab a top-notch executive assistant job with a corporation. I was a fast typist, good with computers and details, and I knew how to deal with demanding bosses. I never thought of going back to Condé Nast.

I wasn't ready to show my work to dealers or curators.

Good painting takes time and immense effort; an artist needs confidence and maturity as well as the technical ability to understand and control the medium. I was working on those issues, but I had a long way to go. The book would give me an unexpected way to save some money for the future.

The next week, after I signed the contract, I told Carrie that I was writing a book and then revealed the title. She raised her pale, plucked eyebrows over the goggle glasses and directed me to apprise her boss about what was going on. Miracle of miracles, the big boss opined that the book was not problematic and the subject matter, which he did not comment on, thank god, didn't present a conflict of interest with my regular column. I returned, hugely relieved, to my cubicle to continue on a piece I'd been working on about an old boxing gym in Greenwich Village.

The gym, it turned out, was the starting point for the book. Its owner was a Damon Runyonesque character named Lenny. Small, intense, and muscled, he was a boxer and a vet with a Marine buzz cut, a Parris Island drill sergeant attitude, and a limp due to the Korean War. Lenny had agreed to cooperate for my article, providing that I worked out at the gym to see what went on there firsthand.

He decreed I would work solely with weights. I wasn't sure I liked the idea. I'd never touched a dumbbell in my life, but I wanted to file an authentic story so I said okay. The gym, on Sheridan Square, looked like a medieval torture chamber to my eyes, which had mostly been exposed to the serenity of a yoga studio.

The second-floor space was musty, sweaty, and dim, with bare lightbulbs hanging in wire cages. Well-worn black rubber mats with curled-up edges were laid out to mute the sound of falling weights but were too thin to do the job. The hard discharge of anger assaulted me when I entered. Lenny gave me the closet off his "office" to change into gray sweats and a navy hoodie. By the time Lenny finished with me that first day, my quads were trembling so hard that I couldn't walk down the two steep flights of stairs without clenching the old wooden banister as if my life depended on it—which I believe it did.

Lenny's last words were, "I'll see you the day after tomorrow."

I wasn't so sure I'd live until then.

But I survived, and thus began a torturous program at the gym. Every so often Lenny let up on me a bit, and I actually came to enjoy him and my hours there. The guys would spot me and help me with the muscle-building contraptions. Ninety percent of the members were gay, gorgeous, megacut, and proud of it. I was once again making new friends—hoping that in a few decades I'd be strong enough to move on to real gloves on the boxing bag.

Eventually I worked up the nerve to ask one of my gym mates, Matt, if he would like to be interviewed for my book. He agreed without hesitation, and we met at a coffee shop a short way from the gym. I was armed with a reporter's notebook and a pen, and I was mute with nervousness.

The word "sex" was not spoken in my family. I hardly ever used it myself. It's only in recent years that I say "fuck" and use the word "motherfucker," regularly and with impunity. But in those years, people used euphemisms like "make love" or "get it on."

I could not look Matt in the eye. I tried small talk but we didn't have that much common ground: he was a gay body builder and I was a heterosexual woman who had never been to a heavy-duty weight-lifting gym before. Finally, I said, "So what is it guys really want in bed?" I simply could not bring myself to say "sex."

And, without a moment's hesitation, he started talking about what I politely wrote down as "oral."

The next several interviews followed the same pattern. It turned out that my gym buddies had absolutely no hesitation in talking about sex to a woman. In fact they *liked* to talk about it—*a lot*. And the straight men I interviewed were no different.

The book was published in 1981 with a huge send-off party at the fabled '21' Club in New York. I was given media training sessions so I wouldn't lower my eyes if I had to utter the word "sex." My coach drilled me on a mantra, "I like this interviewer, I like this interviewer," so I would appear to be friendly and relaxed when, in reality, I didn't give a damn about the interviewer because I was scared as hell.

The coach decreed "clothing appropriate to an authoritative journalist who'd written a book." This meant well-tailored jackets in bright colors that would catch the eye and signal an upbeat personality. My wardrobe in those days consisted of leftover fish market OshKosh's, Levis, army camouflage pants, white shirts from college—all of which were my painting clothes—and the one gray suit I'd worn to the publisher's meeting: I'd given away all my fashionable *Glamour*-era clothing to charity.

A friend suggested her seamstress, who would make three jackets for me at a low price. I found some bright woolens on Orchard Street, where they sell deeply discounted fabric, and ended up with some blazers that I hoped said "authoritative." I wore the brightest one for my first TV interview, with the intimidating Tom Snyder. Thank god it went smoothly.

I had never informed my parents that I was writing the book. Of course I knew they'd find out at some point. On the morning after the Snyder show, my mother phoned me. "I saw you on television last night," she said, and I could hear the icicles dripping through the telephone lines, "and your father and I are so disappointed that you have lost your dignity."

With those words she clicked off. Neither of my parents communicated with me again for well over four years.

My son was now old enough to take the train by himself to Connecticut. He saw his grandparents on weekends when he wasn't with his father or spending time with his friends. For my part, I was honestly relieved not to be in contact with them. In my view, parents are supposed to be supportive and to cheer a child on. Clarkson Potter was a distinguished publishing house, nothing to be ashamed of. Sex and love are part of life. Criticism and disdain are not constructive or nurturing and my parents' comments were painful—once again, I thought, To hell with them.

....

The book was a huge success, largely due to a reviewer at the *Los Angeles Times* whose comment, all these years later, I remember verbatim: "If you look on page 99, your life will be forever changed." It was the beginning of a step-by-step technique on oral sex, aka the blow job.

The book was translated into more than twenty languages. *People* magazine featured a spread of me at Lenny's gym posing, with my biceps curled, on the backs of all the gorgeously muscled guys I had interviewed. I went on a twenty-city publicity tour. The book was on the *New York Times* best-seller list for close to a year! I finally finished my master's degree from Hunter in studio art and art criticism and the big royalty checks let me paint full-time. I could pay half my son's tuition and still have enough to buy myself rolls of high-quality canvas and the best oil paints. I deposited the checks into a savings account at my local bank. The risk of writing a sex book under my own name had paid off.

"What are you doing with all the loot?" asked a friend. When I told him I kept my money in a savings account, he recommended his financial adviser. Apparently, "everyone" in publishing was using him.

The financial adviser reassured me my money would be safe with him and would grow at five or six or more percent—which was a hell of a lot better than what it was making in the bank. I transferred all my earnings to him, except for what I needed to live on.

It was a huge relief not to think about jobs or finances for a while, not to schlep hours to Queens to teach would-be models or to juggle three jobs at once. I could at last concentrate on painting. But almost immediately the publisher was demanding another book.

"Do it," I was urged by the same friend who set me up with the financial adviser. "You can make a lot of money on a follow-up. You'll need it for your old age."

When I thought about his advice that evening, images of bag ladies raced darkly across my mind. I pictured a sad woman trudging through freezing sleet, wet snow, spending marrow-chilling nights in a small room where hard, glittering roaches slithered across bare filthy feet. Strangely, it was then that crushing images like those began regularly to invade my brain without warning—just as I began to finally make more money than what I needed to live on. I didn't stop to figure out where they came from. I knew that I had better make money while I could. There's no security in being an artist. I wrote another book, *How to Make Love to Each Other*. Luckily it was also a best seller.

Now enough royalties were coming in that I needed an accountant. I found someone who was a lawyer as well: he asked to see all my statements from the financial adviser.

"This man is an insurance agent," he said, pointing to small type at the bottom of his statements.

"Yes, I knew that, but I didn't buy insurance from him," I responded.

"He's put you into an insurance fund that is yielding about six percent, which is the good news. The bad news is, his commission is too high and he's also getting a commission from the insurance company. He's being paid twice and that's not kosher in my book. Get out of there."

Little did I ever suspect that this two-bit fraud was a harbinger of much worse things to come.

I asked around and did a ton of homework before transferring my money into one of the most respected investment advisory services in the country. They had a huge research department and a long and distinguished track record in the financial world. They managed the accounts of people who understand money—bankers, venture capitalists, billionaires, trust funders, and their ilk. The manager of my account, Rob, was a very smart guy who sat with me for several hours assessing my financial needs, what kind of risk I could tolerate—almost none—what I could expect to earn in the next ten years —who knows?—and what kind of budget I adhered to—budget? I never had enough money to formulate a budget.

Rob explained that I should understand where my money was invested and how the system worked. My money, he assured me, would be placed in different "instruments"—in other words, it was diversified. I liked him. I trusted him. More important, I trusted the firm that he represented.

At the time, the firm was bullish on Japan and maintained its upbeat attitude until the economy there tanked. And tanked some more. Finally, although I was "diversified," when they pulled out of that mess I had lost about thirty percent of my sex book earnings.

I withdrew what was left and redeposited it in my simple old bank savings account.

CHAPTER 15

What Money Can and Can't Buy

MF + 7 WEEKS

This morning my usual four o'clock wake-up finds me compulsively adding up all the cash I have on hand and reviewing the new AMF budget numbers Tommy helped me draw up. There's not much to work with. My newly developed mental discipline of "no future think" kicks in and I drag myself out of bed to make a cup of coffee.

What can money buy? Coffee! I pour some no-fat cream into the molto-cheap but maximo-delicious espresso that I have substituted for my old-life Dean & DeLuca gourmet blend. Money bought this coffee—but less money than a few months ago—and this pretty porcelain mug. *What can't money buy?* is the next logical question.

I sit down at the computer and take two minutes to list what I think money can and cannot buy. There is something therapeutic about the exercise. I e-mail three friends whom I know wake up early and ask them to send me their inventories.

Alex shoots me back an answer by 6:45 a.m. as the sun's rays sneak onto the keyboard of my laptop.

Here's her response:

Am racing off to the gym but you asked for
off-the-top:
    Above all: Money is Freedom!!! Independence!!
    It can make you feel better. Inspires hope that
things'll get better. Sometimes it brings peace of
mind. It allows you to give more to charity. Help a
friend (tho often bad idea). Provides roof overhead/
won't starve. Sometimes buys influence. It lets you
afford health insurance.
    It can't buy health. Terminal cancer doesn't accept
donations. Can't buy taste—you could hire all stylists/
decorators or whatever and you would remain
tasteless.
    Money cannot ever turn back clock. Cannot buy
wisdom even if you hired all tutors on earth. Can't
make someone love you—no matter how hard you
try. Can't buy talent. Can't buy appreciation for
culture. Can't buy class. Can't buy trust. And at
the risk of widely overstating the obvious, having

$$$ makes you feel a hell of a lot better than not having.

I'm enjoying my second coffee as my friend Patricia Marx's e-mail whistles through the ether. She's an acclaimed humor writer, and I love her words:

If you have money, you can make mistakes and not regret them.

You can make people like you by being generous, which you can do without money, too, but it takes more energy.

In many ways, money buys time, but I bet in the end it doesn't because you have more money-related things to take care of.

Money makes you look better, for sure— clothes, cosmetics, surgical and other kinds of upkeep.

Money and health is a tricky one. It probably doesn't buy you health but if you get sick, you get sick more comfortably and not as unpleasantly.

Money doesn't buy you friends, but it buys you people who'll pretend to be your friends, which might be not so bad.

Money does not buy you good taste or style or brains or talent. I'll do more later, but I'll tell you this now: I'd like enough money to have disdain for it. Xoxxoooxo

A few hours later, another missive arrives from Patty:

Another thing money buys: good lighting, which makes you and your surroundings look better.

Also: help from people you don't have to feel indebted to because you've paid them for their services.

I'm trying to think of what money doesn't buy, and it's a much harder question. However sappy, it's probably true that it doesn't assure you happiness, but it makes unhappiness more pleasant.

Here's the super-quickie from my good friend Richard.

MONEY CAN STILL BUY

Love-in-the-afternoon (or on your lunch break)

Membership at the Ausable Club on Saranac
   Lake

A one-of-a-kind white vicuna suit from Kiton

Your name on the front of the NY Public Library

A week for you and your family at the Villa d'Este
   on Lake Como

MONEY CAN'T BUY

Love

Status

Job security

Height

I call Paul, who refuses to do e-mail, and pose the question. He's an artist and has never had a huge amount of money, but phones me back in a few minutes with his ideas.

"I was thinking a lot about your question and it's an interesting one for me because I'm not very interested in money," he says. "But this is what I think money *can't* buy."

Love

Creativity

Talent

Taste

Peace of mind

Real friends

True admiration

Generosity of spirit

Sincerity

Nurture

Fast reflexes

Sound footing

And sweet dreams

He stops. I wait a second for what money can buy.

"I really love what you just said," I say, and I mean it. I'm very curious as to how he will respond to the second part of my question.

"Money can't buy much," he shoots back immediately when I ask him.

Headaches about money

Porn tapes

And paint

"That's about it," he responds after he's listed those three. The answers are so provocative that I write Carol, a friend in London, for her thoughts. Here's what she e-mails back:

Money cannot make the old young nor the dumb smart nor the short tall nor the black white (or vice versa) nor the disabled whole.

Money cannot make the mad sane nor the wicked good.

Money cannot buy intelligence, genius, or talent (although it can buy competence).

Money cannot buy eternal life.

Money cannot buy you a good, kind, sensitive, empathetic character, nor a joyous personality.

Money cannot buy you a sense of humor or irony.

Money cannot buy you a passionate love of art or nature or the capacity to passionately love another.

Money can buy you everything else.

My friends' answers are sincere and many are clever. My own unedited lists surge out of my unconscious. Sorry, no cheekiness or wit here: I'm too agonized about money these days to make any fun of it. But, come to think of it, maybe the only way to deal with lucre in these economically insane days is to be impudent about it.

MONEY CAN'T BUY

Time

Love

Health

Energy

Talent

Call from my child or my niece

Letter from my grandchild

Freedom

An independent mind

Self-reliance

Real hugs

Loving kisses

A good spirit

Decency

A generous heart

Faith

Hope

Spunk

Courage

Leadership

Can-do attitude

Sincere empathy

Integrity

Reputation

Peace of mind

Equilibrium

Contentment

Body type

An ocean

A star

MONEY CAN BUY

The happiness that comes from travel

Experiences/adventures

Donations to help cure diseases

Fragrance of freesia

Laughter (at a comedy show or movie)

Moonlight

Sunlight

Good teeth

A new hip

Louboutins

Coffee

Chai tea at Starbucks

Manicures

Antique French plates

A great watch

Excitement/adrenaline high

Best medical care

A new heart/liver/kidney

Shelter

Blue eyes (colored contact lenses)

Food

Music

Clothing

Views

Air-conditioning

Heat

A pear tree

Plastic surgery

Hot water

Cameras

Studio

Mosquito netting

Car

Dining out

Picnics

Theater tickets

Popcorn

Television

Computer

Internet access

Christmas trees

Tax attorney

Assisted living

Wine

Good soap

Art

Death (from a Kevorkian-type doctor)

CHAPTER 16

How to Heal a Broken Heart

It was 1983 and our neighborhood had been officially christened SoHo. Busloads of tourists careened down the cobblestone streets snapping photos of artists and local denizens as if they were some species of exotic turtles. Harriet's store downstairs was doing a land-office business and my sales help on Saturdays was needed more than ever. Across from my small space on West Broadway was Mr. Kochendorfer's knife-sharpening business. His father sat on a chair outside the front door carefully surveying the scene from a black peeling-leather office chair that rolled around on rusty casters. On one side of him was an enormous, cavernous building with greasy yellowing tile walls, a garage for garbage trucks. Its huge doors crashed down with colossal *kabaaaangs* after the hump-backed garbage trucks rumbled grumpily out onto the street at three a.m. every day.

On the other side of Mr. Kochendorfer was a well-architected nineteenth-century building. It wasn't a cast-iron beauty like many in the neighborhood, but it had an appealing facade, huge windows, and very high ceilings. I could see into it from my place and it seemed the perfect abode for a painter and her son. I daydreamed about buying a loft in that building, and even received a generous offer for a loan from my old landlord and friend, Arthur, for a down payment, but I didn't want to be indebted to anyone.

I wrote yet a third book on love and relationships and it, too, did well financially. Despite my losses in the Japanese market, my savings from book advances and royalties were more substantial than I could have predicted possible a couple years ago. I stayed in our small space and life went on smoothly and uneventfully with unimportant ups and downs. My son was applying to colleges and I finished the third book, went on some unremarkable blind dates, wrote a few articles on art criticism, did freelance writing, and reaped good fees from start-up-magazine consulting. I spent a long, food-oriented summer in Tuscany with a girlfriend who had rented a villa there and enjoyed several vacation trips to France and Spain. At home, I grew somewhat discouraged about finding a gallery but I kept on making art. It was the only work I really loved—then and now.

I had a new circle of friends—artists, dancers, writers, poets, shopkeepers, knife-grinders. Often in the evenings I heard a pebble strike my window, thrown from the street below.

"You busy?" a friend would call out.

"C'mon up for a drink," I'd say, throwing down the keys, wrapped in an old sock, to their outstretched hands so they could join me at my recently acquired, much-cherished refectory table. I always kept a bottle of good Chianti and chilled Pinot Grigio on hand, and usually had some superb, freshly made smoky mozzarella from Freddy's Dairy on Sullivan Street in the fridge. If my day had taken me by Mr. Dappolito's bakery a couple of blocks away, I would have a semolina loaf right out of his bakery oven. Bread, wine, and cheese have always been a perfect meal to me. They never tasted better than in my small West Broadway place.

By 1987, my son had left for college and the streets of SoHo were even more packed with tourists. When I walked out the door of my home, I felt as though I were in a jam-packed rush-hour subway train. The throng was at its noisiest on weekends when I was trying to paint and think. The neighborhood had become a shoppers' paradise, but to me it was hell. It was time to move.

With the proceeds from the books, I bought my first piece of real estate, a one-bedroom apartment in Greenwich Village near my old college-days haunt, Washington Square. Prices in SoHo had escalated so much that I couldn't afford a loft on a quieter street, but this would be a solid investment in a good location. Owning my own apartment gave me a new feeling of well-being and security. I reasoned that my son would soon be off on his own and I could work in a small alcove off the bedroom, as I had begun doing very small-scale paintings and collages. Someday, if I saved more money, I would rent a good-size studio.

I loved being in a quiet, safe building with a doorman and a super who doubled as a much-needed handyman. I even had enough money to get my old friend, designer Larry Totah, to help decorate, and together we painted the walls a pale sienna, which reminded me of Italy. A silky apricot rug adorned my bedroom, and a new down-cushioned sofa slip-covered in natural linen was a focal point in the minimalist living room. We installed all new appliances in the small but efficient galley kitchen, but left the classic black-and-white tile floor.

Inexplicably, even owning my own apartment, the bag lady anxieties lurked. I had finally called my parents and visited them in Connecticut, but our relationship remained chilly and removed. My son was away at school, and I wished I could find the right man and often wondered if I were doing something to sabotage myself in the relationship department. I questioned whether I really had the goods as an artist. I didn't know where my life was going. I also wanted to get rid of the fiendish, unreal fears of being a bag lady, so I decided that I needed a shrink to help me look honestly at my self. I asked around and found a well-regarded therapist whom I began seeing once a week.

About a year later, I found myself lying on the kitchen floor in my apartment, my entire body rigid with pain and fear and dread and defeat. I tried with all my will to think my way out of this paralysis, but my brain could only tap out codes of unbearable anxiety. The telephone was lying next to my ear and I finally picked it up.

"Is there any chance I can see you this afternoon or to-morrow morning, or even tomorrow afternoon?" I entreated Dr. R, the therapist I'd been seeing. "I really need to meet with you as soon as possible." My hands were trembling so violently that the phone fell from my grip. Surely the doctor would detect the panic in my voice. There was a pause and I heard the faintest sound of shuffling of pages.

"I'm very sorry," Dr. R said. "Unfortunately, I have no time until your regular appointment on Friday. If you need me you can always phone. If I'm not here, the service will take your message."

Just as Dr. R hung up, my call waiting clicked and a voice said, "AP—AP? Are you there? It's Lynn."

"I'm here. Hi, how are you?" I heard myself saying. I worked on writing projects for Lynn. It was imperative that I pull myself together enough to discuss the piece she was calling about.

"You don't sound good," Lynn said, not missing a beat. "Is there anything the matter?"

"I'm not really so good." The words just spilled out. "I was just speaking to my shrink. Something's come up and I needed to see him and he blew me off for four days—"

"Who are you seeing?" she interrupted. I told her the doctor's name.

"For god's sake, he's not for you, he's doesn't know how to deal with creative people. Forget him. You've got to call Dr. J. He's worked with some great writers and artists and you will love him. Here's his number. Do you have a piece of paper?"

"I don't think I should call another doctor while I'm seeing Dr. R . . ." I said dubiously, still lying on the floor.

"That's nonsense!" Lynn assured me. "Here's his number. His office is on Lexington Avenue. Call him as soon as we hang up. You must promise me you will do this. Dr. R won't be able to help you. I happen to know about him. He's one of those Freudian types who makes you lie down and babble on and on and he never says a word. He is not right for you. Please do this, please see Dr. J."

"Okay," I said at last, so I could end the conversation. But she insisted that I find a piece of paper to take down the number before I hung up.

I don't know how long I was on the tile floor. An hour? Two? More? Who cared about time? I didn't care about anything. I was grateful that my brain had shifted into neutral; I just stayed there doing nothing but counting the tiles that I could see from my crammed-in position between the two rows of cabinets. I counted and recounted the tiles dozens—no hundreds—of times. Then I memorized Dr. J's number and address. I repeated those numbers like a mantra.

I don't know what made me lift the receiver and dial Dr. J's office. A strong pleasant voice answered, "This is Dr. J."

At six thirty that evening I was sitting in a chair opposite Dr. J, a tall, silver-haired, distinguished-looking man, past president of the American Psychoanalytic Association. At the time he was seventy-five. The first thing I noticed were his eyes, which were the intense blue color of the sky on an early summer morning. He wore an impeccable gray suit, starched white shirt, small gold cufflinks, and polished black shoes. There was an ineffable, comforting quality to him: I knew at first glance that this was a man who had seen it all.

"You can sit here next to me, or use that if you want," he said with a warm smile, when I pointed to the ubiquitous leather-covered couch that graced all the offices of the shrinks I'd read about or seen in movies.

Dr. J's warmth and immediately empathetic manner made it easy to talk. I heard myself telling him that I'd finally met a man named F whom I thought I was in love with. He had abruptly broken things off when we began talking about living together and he wouldn't return my phone calls. My reaction was so extreme that I couldn't function. Dr. J asked me to tell him briefly about my background and the difficult relationship with my parents and the bag lady fears I'd alluded to. About an hour and a half later, I heard the diagnosis—"a broken sense of self" and "a broken heart"—and the words "I'd like to see you again tomorrow. Can you come at seven fifteen in the morning?"

I could have wept with gratitude, but I was cried out from the hour and a half that I had spent recounting my life story and how I had found myself shaped like an overly fried doughnut on my black-and-white kitchen floor.

He walked me to his walnut-paneled office door, took my hand in his two warm ones, and said, "I'll be the last doctor on the case." I believed him absolutely.

Over the three years that I saw Dr. J I was to find out that even though I was a highly functioning person professionally, my heart, my soul, and my self were all broken long before I ever met the charming, brilliant, handsome, witty, undependable F. Not surprisingly, most of it had to do with my childhood.

CHAPTER 17

Real Estate Woes

MF + 2 MONTHS

Two months and counting since I was MF'd. It's February and I have returned to Florida, still trying to sell the cottage. My publisher has put me on a strict deadline, and I am grateful for the chance to write my book here and to wake up to clear blue skies and splashing sunshine. Everyday living is much cheaper in this part of the country. And there are no New York distractions.

The Realtor arranged for an open house a few days ago. Five people dropped by; two were neighbors who live on the street, curious to know what the place looked like from the inside. An open house for brokers was scheduled for a week later; two agents showed up. Three years ago when I bought the place there was a feeding frenzy of buyers and brokers because so little was on the market. Now there are four FOR

SALE signs on my short three-block street. The rest of the area, middle- to lower-middle-class, is littered with signs advertising foreclosures, "bank owned," and "short sale," a euphemism for another form of "foreclosure."

This neighborhood, safe as a bank vault less than a year ago, has witnessed several high-noon robberies at gunpoint. Crimes have multiplied like amoebas. Two single women, a block away from where I sit right now, returned home for lunch and caught sight of two burglars, handguns stuffed behind their belts, in their kitchen packing the loot into garbage bags. The house had been ransacked but they were very lucky; the robbers high-tailed it as soon as the owners stepped in the door.

I had signed up for electronic surveillance when I purchased the house, but of course after being MF'd I've stopped the service. And no one's buying. So I'm back here to try to drum up some sales interest and to meet my deadline. I'm now typing in a friend's kitchen because I feel insecure and jumpy in broad daylight inside a once-sweet-and-safe house.

This economic meltdown seemed to be as unexpected as an ice storm on the equator, and the freeze in Florida is especially severe. The entrepreneurial Central and South Americans who settled in this midsection of the state started a variety of small businesses: landscaping, bakeries, restaurants, plumbing, painting, carpentry, house-cleaning services. As homeowners sink into bankruptcy, these trades are hit hard. People let their lawns and weeds grow, they cook at home, they clean their own houses. They're hunkering down, fearful of their own futures, trying not to spend money and frantic about mortgages, car payments, and credit card debt. President Obama has just signed a bill to help homeowners but from what I'm reading and hearing it's just a start. Much more is needed. There's no mortgage on my little cottage in Florida so I can't rely on the government to help out.

....

Of course my highly mortgaged Long Island place is on the market, too. No takers there either. When the bag lady fears attack at four a.m., I panic that neither of the houses will ever sell.

And then there's my studio. I looked for almost a year for a safe, pleasant space to do my photography, which had taken the place of painting. Working full-time in my apartment became impossible when I began to use the oversize machines and computers I needed for prints that measured six or seven feet. I had become increasingly anxious and depressed about my work, which was at a standstill because searching for the right space at the right price had become such an obsession with me. A friend suggested a consultant who specialized in work and career issues. I told her that I'd located a small and wonderful space that was far more than I wanted to spend.

She was smart and pragmatic. "Even though the price is high and it's not as large as you would like, take the space because you feel good in it and you will do good work there," she said. "Focus on creating and selling your flower prints for three days a week. Use the rest of your time to explore the work you love, the plastic dolls. And always keep in mind that being an artist includes having to sell work."

I hate having to hustle to sell work. So does almost every other artist and writer who walks the planet. We just want to work flat out. No interruptions. No having to deal with money, no trying to find someone to buy pictures, no calling galleries that don't call you . . .

Ah, but I'm whining. Who on the planet would not want to be free to do as he or she pleases? I should delete all those belly-aching words—right now. Yet I don't think I will. I can't pretend I don't have moments like these. I took the career consultant's advice and met with an accountant who agreed I would have to sell a lot of work to make the studio a legitimate enterprise, but he thought it was a risk worth taking. I ended up in a fine SoHo building, with great light, half the amount of space I would have liked, and two and a half times the rent I had in mind. But it made me happy—and happiness is a uniquely precious commodity.

I signed the documents knowing I would have to borrow from the home equity account to pay what I owed each month for the studio's upkeep. It was one of the two or three biggest personal and financial gambles that I have ever made. But for the first two years of the lease it paid off: I sold enough photographs to cover the rent and the costs of very expensive paper and archival inks as well as the pricey insurance required by the landlord.

Now an expensive year is left on the lease; I've had no luck negotiating my top-tier rent. The managing agent is a chilly piece of work. Rents are falling substantially everywhere around me in SoHo. Still, I'm obligated to pay the rent under the lease and the threat of a lawsuit for defaulting is something I do not need. I've never defaulted on anything. I'm not going to start now.

I will keep this studio! I will work harder than I ever have before—which was pretty hard indeed—and see what happens. I have the feeling something good will come of it: tough, challenging work and laserlike focus have always paid off for me. In the past, unexpected opportunities have materialized at just the right moment. It's said that "lucky" people put themselves in good fortune's path, and I think that's true. If I keep working and thinking positively, my luck will turn.

CHAPTER 18

The Pink Ribbon

In the summer of 1989, I was writing another book and continuing my consulting work. But as a freelancer I was thinking of the uncertainty of the future and spoke often to Dr. J about my bag lady fears and how deep-rooted those anxieties werc.

I had just returned from a long July Fourth weekend in Florida. Two friends and I had stayed at the guesthouse of my old Boss of Bosses from Condé Nast and his captivating and scholarly wife.

The days in Florida were sunny and hot with magnificent white billowing clouds against a brilliant, endless blue sky, and every morning we walked on the miles-long white-sand beach, pairing off so we could catch up on each other's news. The boss and I talked about my books, the television talk-show series I was working on about women's issues, and, of course, magazines, including one that he was having particular problems with, *Self.* In the evening we all watched a Jean Renoir movie and headed off early to be lullabied to sleep by the ocean waves just a few feet away.

On Sunday morning, about seven, I opened the door of the guesthouse and on the front step were copies of the New York newspapers for the three of us who were staying there. Tucked into my *New York Times* was an issue of *Self* magazine. The highest-priced delivery boy on the planet had placed it there. I knew he wanted to know what I thought of his troubled publication.

I skimmed the paper, read *Self* cover to cover, and automatically began jotting down some notions that might improve the cover and some story ideas—shades of decades ago when I'd placed a memo about what was wrong with *Vogue* in his old office in-box.

I gave my notes to the Boss of Bosses when we came home for lunch after our morning walk. I had no ulterior motives. I very much liked the idea of a magazine for smart women, which was how *Self* had originated. From what he'd said at the beach and from what I'd seen in the magazine itself, I could understand how it had lost its bearings and I simply thought I had some ideas that might be useful. Nothing more was said about my notes until Monday when, back in New York, I received a call from a mutual acquaintance saying that the Boss of Bosses thought I might be interested in being the editor of *Self* magazine.

I responded, as graciously as possible, that I couldn't

possibly take on such a job with all my other serious commitments and, in addition, I didn't want to go back to the magazine world again.

"Don't be foolish," the friend chided me. "This is a major job. An important job. Do not give me an answer now. Sleep on it and call me in the morning."

I agreed to give the offer serious consideration but I really wasn't interested, even though I remained nervous about the future. Having a steady job with what I was sure would be a high salary and fabulous perks was delicious to contemplate, but I had been there, done that, and quit to work as a fishmonger. It wasn't my kind of life. I was doing well with books, I owned my apartment, I had a shot at a television series, and in a couple of years I might be able to find a studio of my own and begin serious painting once again.

I called the go-between early the next morning and said it was the most tempting offer that I could imagine but I had to turn it down.

"What would it take for you to say yes? Everyone has a number. I'm sure you have one, too. Why don't you call me back and let me know," he said.

That afternoon I gave him a crazy beyond-the-beyond number that I was sure would be laughed off as a big joke, and within forty-eight hours I was signing a contract to be the editor of *Self* magazine. Several months later I ran into someone who had been privy to what had happened behind the scenes.

"That was a brilliant negotiating technique," she said. "You had them right where you wanted them."

I laughed. "What are you talking about, 'technique'? I really didn't want the job."

"That's the best bargaining position of all," she said. Interesting, isn't it, how distance and unavailability can make something or someone so desirable. And interesting how life can take such unexpected turns. Here I was, going back to Condé Nast years after quitting *Glamour* to become an artist. I liked my life, but the artist's or freelancer's existence is almost always a two-sided one: I had day-to-day freedom but I was consistently in a precarious financial position, always pitching ideas for the next writing job, thinking up the next book idea, and hoping against hope my work would interest a dealer in New York.

I was still seeing Dr. J when I took the new job. We both recognized the irony of my being the editor of *Self* magazine while I was trying to construct a strong new self of my own. Of course I spoke to him often of the largely judgmental role my parents had played in my life. I thought that telling my parents about my new job would be a good way to let them know I wasn't a dirty-book writer anymore.

"Oh, hello dear," my mother said, as if I'd been in touch with her ten minutes before. I told her about my new position.

"It sounds very nice, dear. You'll have a great deal of responsibility and you must make sure to take care of your health," she said, adding, "Such a shame it isn't *Vogue*."

On a Thursday at seven thirty a.m.—not even twenty-four hours after I signed the contract—I reported for work at *Self*. I had wanted to wait until Monday so I could tie up loose ends before starting a demanding job, but I had forgotten the Condé Nast code of urgency. I agreed that I must start immediately!

I entered the glass doors of the Condé Nast building, which was then on Madison Avenue, wearing a strictly business gray flannel Chanel suit (first clothing allowance purchase, half an hour after signing the contract), low-heeled Manolos (didn't have enough time to hustle over to Bergdorf to buy the editorially de rigueur four-inch stilettos), and my black Hermès Kelly purse (the only thing I'd kept from my *Glamour* magazine days).

At the newsstand in the lobby, I bought a *Wall Street Journal,* which I felt was required in order to glean some understanding of what was transpiring in the world of business. The Condé Nast newsstand was more like an elite bookstore with pricey titles for fashion and beauty and travel magazines from Europe, Asia, Australia, China, Japan, Russia, and even India. I pulled out a dollar for the *Journal* and the tall, sandy-haired man standing at the rack nearest me politely asked my name in what sounded vaguely like a German accent. I told him, rather surprised that he wanted to know.

"You have a charge account here," he said.

"No, I think there's a mistake, this is the first time I've bought a paper from you."

"Word came down from on high." He rolled his pale blue eyes behind their colorless Andy Warhol frames skyward. "You're the new editor. All the chiefs just choose anything they want. It's all yours."

"Well, thank you very very much," I said. This was my first encounter with the many fabulous editorial privileges that were to follow.

I consulted the directory for *Self*'s floor, entered the elevator, pressed 21, and when the doors opened I had no idea where to go. Out of the ether a person from Personnel appeared (how did she divine I was in the elevator?) and led me to an airy, windowed office at least four times the size of Miss G's, with its own private bathroom. I also had been assigned a decorating budget, a wildly generous clothing allowance, plus a slinky, shiny black car with a Russian ex-KGB driver.

My first executive decision was where to hang three very small paintings I had brought with me. I had done them years ago and they would go on the inside door of my shiny white-tiled bathroom so I wouldn't forget who I was. It was easy to see how that could happen, being treated like this every day.

I walked over to the table that had been placed in the middle of the room and tugged it over to a corner were I could look out the window at the New York skyline. I was beginning to realize what I was facing, the enormity of my task. I'd never edited an entire magazine before, much less one that needed a lot of help. Since Phyllis Wilson, the founding editor, had died, readers had signaled their dissatisfaction: subscription numbers had fallen, advertising was off, and newsstand sales were way down. The Boss of Bosses had signed me on to fix this.

The good news was that the *Self* staff was very smart, super smart, smart beyond measure. My office door was guarded by Judy Kent, whose brain could outwit fifty mainframe computers. Up to now, my weekly housekeeper and a sometime bookkeeper had been my only "staff." I had to learn—urgently—how to manage about ninety people. I can't begin to count the mistakes I made.

Slowly, the magazine began to attract new readers and old subscribers renewed. We focused on health and fitness, which were *Self*'s birthright. I thought of Phyllis daily as I sat at a long, antique refectory table in my redecorated version of her office. She actually had bought the excerpt from *How to Make Love to a Man,* as she had promised to do all those years ago. She had become a friend and I had seen her and her husband, Hugh, often. Phyllis was highly cerebral, a no-nonsense woman who had begun her career at *Vogue* as a writer. She was a New Orleans girl, and we would often sip cocktail sherry from small etched antique glasses that she had brought from her genteel Southern life, in the sitting room of her brownstone apartment, swapping magazine news and gossip.

As I recall, it was almost immediately after convincing the Boss of Bosses to start a new magazine that Phyllis was diagnosed with breast cancer. Throughout the chemo and radiation, she was at her desk—she disdained the "silliness of worktables"—poring over every article that went into the magazine, attending every meeting, working on every layout with the Art department and continuing nonstop on weekends. She never mentioned her illness and worked until it was no longer possible for her to be brought into the office. Phyllis was a role model to all of us who knew her.

During the time I was editing *Self*, I was keeping a close watch on government spending on women's health. Hardworking advocacy groups had helped to expand dollars that went into AIDS research while breast cancer received less. According to the National Institutes of Health, by 1989 the government was spending $74.5 million on breast cancer annually, and over $2 billion on HIV/AIDS, although breast cancer killed more than 40,000 women in 1989 as compared with 22,000 AIDS patients in the same year. This was an outrage, as research in those years was showing that one in nine women would be diagnosed with breast cancer.

AIDS activists had developed the powerful symbol of a red ribbon, which I wore on my lapel. I was passionate about finding a symbol that would be as equally influential and conspicuous as the red ribbon. The staff, of course, was aware of the ravages of this cancer and my deep interest in doing something in memory of Phyllis and for the women who had been struck by the disease.

On a fine late spring morning, Nancy Smith, one of the super-duper smarties, burst into my office with the news that a woman in Arizona had created a peach-colored ribbon for breast cancer awareness.

"Let's get her on the phone right away and tell her we want to cooperate with her and make the ribbon into a national symbol," I said. "We have the power of over two million smart and caring readers who will get behind this." But the peach ribbon lady wasn't interested in our entreaties.

I mulled over what to do throughout the morning. I called the Condé Nast lawyers and asked them if it would be okay to create a pink ribbon even if there already was a colored ribbon for breast cancer awareness out there. Yes, it was fine, they reported back, it would not conflict with the Arizona ribbon. I called the Boss of Bosses and asked to see him right away. Super urgent!

"I'd like to attach an actual pink ribbon to the magazine's cover to go with a major story we're doing on breast cancer," I said.

He listened but then explained why the idea wasn't feasible in terms of cost and printing.

"How about binding a ribbon into the inside of the magazine on our editorial pages?"

Same problem.

"What about binding in just a very thin pink thread?" I kept pressing. But it just wasn't practical.

I returned to my office. The pink ribbon had to be launched in a major way to have a significant impact on breast cancer awareness. It was then that I remembered that Evelyn Lauder was becoming a well-known advocate for fighting the disease. Mrs. Lauder would see me right away, her assistant Margaret replied when I phoned.

I actually ran over to the office of *Self*'s publisher, Larry Burstein, and nervily barged into a meeting he was presiding over. This was the Everest of urgency! We were on a killer deadline. Literally. Women were dying every day from the disease and thousands were being diagnosed.

Larry had sworn to the code of urgency and was kind

enough to listen to what I had to say, despite my rude interruption. He was a million percent behind the idea and
dismissed the meeting. Two minutes later we grabbed our
coats, piled into my black Condé Nast car that was always on
call, and directed the ex-KGB driver to the GM building.

Larry and I outlined the plan to Evelyn: the October issue of the magazine would do an in-depth portfolio on the
latest developments in research and treatment for the disease.
I asked if she would like to be the guest editor of the special
section. In addition, we told her about the pink ribbon and
asked if she would consider allowing us to place a glass bowl
with pink ribbons, handmade by the *Self* staff, on Estée
Lauder counters in New York stores.

"I'll do you one better," she said without a nanosecond's
hesitation. "We'll put the ribbons on every Lauder counter
across the country!"

The rest, as they say, is history. *Self* magazine launched
the pink ribbon in October 1992. Evelyn is the one who made
the pink ribbon for breast cancer awareness a global symbol.
She is responsible for saving the lives of thousands and thousands of women. Phyllis Wilson would honor her as a true
heroine. So would legions of others here at home and around
the world.

Without the Boss of Bosses there would be no pink ribbon, and he deserves real credit as well. The impact and
effectiveness of the pink ribbon was something that was
achieved only through many activists and the power of an
established publication with millions of intelligent readers. I
was immensely grateful for the chance to help so many

women. In the end, *Self* magazine was indeed a keystone in building a new self of my own.

....

During the years I edited *Self,* I was making what I considered an astronomical salary and salting away every cent I could. I felt like a rich person for the first—and only—time in my life. Here was my first real lesson in what money *could* buy! I had a car and driver, clothes, jewels, orchids, money to throw great parties, and lots to spend on exotic, luxurious travel. I mostly worked seven days a week, with business breakfasts, business lunches, and business dinners. Work was so inextricably woven into what I thought of as "real life" that I couldn't tell the difference between the two. I met fascinating people and had adventures and experiences that no other job would have given me.

One thing I never lost sight of: though I was sitting in an elegant and expensive—but rented—chair at my Condé Nast antique table, the rich days there would not last forever.

I had finished my sessions with Dr. J. I felt strong and confident but restless. I had talked at length with him about leaving my job to go back to a more independent creative existence, even though it was far less secure financially. I understood that over the years of my professional life, I had always survived—and succeeded—and now I felt resilient and much more equipped psychologically to be on my own again. I made my decision and scheduled an appointment with the Boss of Bosses and we mutually agreed that I had accomplished my mission. After seven years of hard work, in 1996, the magazine was on a steady course, revenues had escalated, readers renewed their subscriptions, newsstand sales were healthy, and I wanted to return to some form of creating art. What that form was I didn't know. I had, over the years, lost my passion for painting. I knew deep down I wasn't good enough to be the kind of painter that I wanted to be.

I became a well-paid freelancer, consulting on magazines and Web site development to make money, but I was, for four years, in an uncomfortable free fall when it came to what I really wanted to do. At the same time, inexplicably, the bag lady fears were on the rise. I had been regularly contributing to my IRA and I had some money left in my bank savings account. I bought the little house on Long Island with a small down payment and a large mortgage, thinking that it would be a good investment if those fears ever materialized. I thought of consulting Dr. J again, but he had long since retired to Florida.

On Christmas Day 1998, Paul, whom I'd been seeing for a couple years, gave me a present he'd received in a charity takeaway goody bag. It was a blue-and-gray plastic digital camera, worth about thirty bucks. It weighed less than a stick of butter and was such a primitive little thing that it didn't even have a screen on the back so you could see what picture you were taking. The digital cameras I use now can be up to 22 megapixels and even more. My little plastic Intel camera was just half of a single megapixel.

I adored that simple camera far more than I would have loved a twenty-five-carat flawless D diamond. I took thousands of pictures with it. Everything looked better through its tiny eyepiece: the sky was bluer, the ocean greener, the waves whiter. Flowers had the most ravishing colors. The world is gorgeous when you look through a lens. The final pictures took time and effort but they didn't take years of trying to control beautiful but intransigent oil paints. I felt the results from a camera were far more exciting and satisfying than painting. Thanks to Paul's gift, I had stumbled on the medium that was made for me.

The little camera took possession of me. I bought eleven more on eBay over the years and I still use some of them to this day. Of course I wanted to print my work, so I had to learn how to operate complex printers the size of a living room sofa. The effort of mastering Photoshop to manipulate my photographs was worthy of a doctorate degree. I spent six long and fruitful years understanding the technology, working from a room I'd converted into a studio in the lovely new apartment that I'd moved to during my magazine days. I had searched the Village for something where I could do more entertaining, but nothing seemed right. My new apartment with its sweeping East River views was luxurious and much larger than my Village place. It had been the perfect setting to give business dinners but the best part was having a sunny extra room in which to do my photography. I loved getting up in the morning, drinking my coffee, and not having to dress for work. My "studio" was ten feet away and it was perfect for the relatively small flower prints I was making at the time, but I was soon to outgrow it.

CHAPTER 19

What Can I Live Without?

MF + 9 WEEKS

Yesterday, Saturday, I was feeling upbeat and optimistic here in Florida until I received an e-mail from Louise, a good friend, informing me she'd been laid off the day before. At two in the afternoon she was told to clean out her desk and depart the premises by four p.m. Twenty percent of the staff was sacked in the same inhumane way. She is the eleventh person I know who's been fired in the last few weeks.

Louise is a sexy elegant woman in her mid-fifties, an award-winning graphics designer at the top of her profession. Although her publication was suffering from decline in ad revenue and newsstand sales like everyone else in the business, it was nevertheless a shock when the company announced a major downsizing to concentrate on building up its net presence. Younger, less highly paid people will absorb her job.

The week before, her husband, a quiet, brainy guy, a published writer, and an editor at one of the top publishing houses, was also unceremoniously let go. He had been hired with great fanfare and a major salary to start his own imprint there only six months ago. I phone her immediately.

"I don't know what will happen to us," she says, in an eerily quiet voice. "We won't be able to pay the rent on this place. Our savings can last us a year at most. We had a small amount of money in the market, and less than half is left. I wanted to buy bonds but the broker convinced me that blue chips would do better and be safe. And, of course, they went down with everything else. I am so staggered by this, I can't even think. We'll be out on the streets."

I know exactly how she feels. I am at a loss about how to help, but at last an idea comes. She can use my studio until I sell the Florida house and am back up north. It will give her a place to go and think clearly—I know that is something I needed desperately in the first few weeks post-MF. We discuss the possibility of freelancing, designing books, writing books, even working in a bookstore as a salesclerk.

"Thank god I was tops in a secretarial course I took," she says, trying to lighten the mood, and falling flat. "I can enter data into a computer at six bucks an hour."

She is fifty-five and may never find another position at her present level in publishing. It is even possible that she may not find a job for years. She can consider becoming a sales-person, or a real estate agent, or a cosmetics hawker, but every-one else who's been laid off is looking for the same kinds of jobs. And what about the years of experience that she may never use again? Will she and her husband have to leave New York and go back to Pittsburgh, where they are both from? I have an acute pain in my gut for the sleepless nights she will have to endure.

Yesterday I also received an e-mail from a writer friend, Marcy, who knows about my bag lady fears, explaining her own situation:

> I'm 100% in the market. The money from my book advance was in my bank account and then when everyone got panicked about having more than $100,000 in the bank, I asked my guy if I should get a T-bill or city bond or something like that. And he said he thought that was a bad idea, that he had something safer or better. I really wasn't paying attention.
>
> When he asked do I need money immediately, I said no but I might need it toward the end of the year if I want to buy a country place, so leave some out so I could use it for that.
>
> He now says I never said that. So he put the $100,000 in the market. The other day, I e-mailed him (he's in Calif) and asked whether he had a strategy other than wait it out, and he basically said wait it out.

> And he said nothing's safe. It makes me sick, but I just
> try not to think about it.

Like me, my writer, editor, and painter friends depend on and trust "experts" to take care of what money we may have. Marcy's e-mail got me thinking.

Were our decisions bad? Were we wrong to trust other people with our fortunes? Were we so focused on other things in our lives that we simply "didn't pay attention"?

This is the kind of thinking that gets you into trouble, but it's almost impossible to avoid. You start thinking backward and examining all the decisions you made, or didn't make. You lament that you followed this path instead of that. You start with the "if only"s. Regret, to me, is a big waste of valuable time. It can't turn back the clock and only serves to make you more anxious and upset. I slap it down whenever it rears its devious little head.

When I made the decision to give my money to the MF in 1999, I did my homework. I was wary after my experience with the financial adviser/insurance agent who was double-dipping with his fees, and then with the highly regarded fund that invested in Japan. I checked out the MF with smart money people who had also invested with him. Ditto financial advisers who seemed envious that I was in the elite Madoff club.

My novelist friend also did some background checking on the recommendation she had received: Her financial guy worked with many other writers, and the lawyer she's depended on for years as a sounding board approved her decision. Does she regret putting her money with him?

No, she tells me, she doesn't. And for the same reason I don't regret my decision. Our judgment calls, based on the information we had at the time, were right at the time we made them.

"All the knowledge I had last year pointed to investing with him," she tells me when we meet for an early dinner at our favorite place, EJ's Luncheonette. "I have learned not to second-guess my past and hang out with my regrets. It's a waste of emotional and mental energy that can be used for other things."

"Like trying to stay thin," I interject.

"Yes," she says as she orders her usual: an egg white and basil omelet, "no butter on it, please, no bread, no potatoes." She weighs all of 103 pounds including the black jeans she has on tonight.

We both laugh.

Usually we trade work stories and chat about what we've checked out on eBay, but tonight we're in a philosophical mood. We're "creative" people, we've been successful at what we do. And now, like everyone else, we suddenly find ourselves in a completely new world.

We start ruminating about "success" and what it is. Meanwhile, I am debating whether to order the carrot cake, which, at EJ's, is incredibly delicious, especially the butter-cream frosting. Two warnings skitter across my mind: No, don't do it, you've been "good" and had a boring but low-calorie egg white omelet like Marcy. No, you should not spend three more dollars. You just had all your money stolen!

I defiantly order the carrot cake and ask, "So what separates successful and not successful people?"

"We all face setbacks," Marcy replies. "We're all going to get jolted. Good or bad, something is going happen to you. It's life and it happens to you. If you don't accept what's happened—like your thing with the MF—you're just having a tantrum like a two-year-old, and what good will it do you? A 'successful' person adjusts to the situation and presses on."

"Yes," I say. "We're talking here about being successful as a human being, not necessarily being 'successful' in Wall Street terms."

"What other way would you want to be successful? Sure, it's important to have money. I'm talking here about people who are not defeated by setbacks," Marcy replies. "My guess is that those kind of people will also be financially comfortable, but not necessarily rich."

The carrot cake is a dream. The calories are a nightmare. Wouldn't it be great to order a second one—just this one time? I think.

"It's about self-control and discipline," I say, finally nixing the idea of more cake. "You just can't allow yourself to wallow in your problems. You suck it up. Get on with it."

"One other thing," Marcy says. I am wildly envious she has left half of the egg white omelet on EJ's beige oval plate. "If something bad happens I always think it's 'life' or rotten luck. I don't take it personally."

"That's the only attitude to have," I agree.

We split the check, leaving a big tip because we've been there for hours and the waitress has been giving us nonstop free refills. I take a last look at my spotless plate. I've broken my diet, but "No regrets!" I remind myself sternly.

Nevertheless the next morning I wake up bemoaning my carrot cake indulgence and I begin thinking what would happen if I could never eat another peanut butter cookie or my all-time favorite, bread and butter. What could I live without?

It's five thirty a.m., raining hard, too early to head to the studio, so I make a second cup of coffee and start jotting down lists on the back of an envelope that had contained a credit card solicitation:

CAN'T LIVE WITHOUT

Family and friends and a roof over my head

Health insurance

Regular mammograms and checkups

Work

A new computer every four to five years

BlackBerry

Cameras and printers

Regular teeth-cleanings

Kyle, my colorist

Brand-name vodka [I'm not a big drinker but
    I like to offer friends the best I can afford]

Diet Dr Pepper

Eating Japanese food once in a while

A clean and tidy space around me

Bread [crusty Italian] and butter

Seeing an ocean

The warmest goose-down jacket

Good, long-lasting soap

A party—once in a while

A good pedicure—once in a while

Books and probably Netflix

One no-iron white shirt a year from Lands' End

CAN LIVE WITHOUT

Morning anxiety demons

Carrot cake

A getaway house

Luxury cosmetics

Premium TV

Blow-drys for special occasions

Cut flowers, although almost every time I pass
    the corner deli with its displays of tulips
    and roses I wish I could buy a bunch

Manicures

90 percent of dry-cleaning

Fax machine

Charge cards [except one for emergency use
    only]

Gourmet food shops

Prada et al.

FedEx [which I used a lot]

Impulse purchases, no matter how small

Exotic travel [but I'll miss it a lot]

More shoes, bags, antique china, sheets

Shopping, except for necessities

Car

Overpriced coffee

Magazine subscriptions

eBay

Botox [this is last because I may relent]

CHAPTER 20

What the Bag Lady Really Fears

D r. J was the first person I spoke openly with about my bag lady nightmares. In the months after I came out of the bag lady closet I compared notes with many other women who described their own losing-it-all dreads. Sufferers ranged from age twenty-five to upward of sixty, they were married or single, some were mothers or grandmothers, many were successful career women, some had remained home to take care of children and were intending to return to the workplace.

The visual images we all harbor were surprisingly similar and vivid. Only the details of living circumstances and physical condition differed individually. The majority of us agreed that our most deeply felt fear was that we would lose our autonomy and would forever live in utter poverty.

Here's the full spectrum of bag lady anxieties that I listed for Dr. J. I feared that I would:

Lose my independence and control over my life

Lose my dignity

Be alone and abandoned

Lose my identity

Lose social status

Have people pity me

End up impoverished on cold and icy streets

Lose all hope

What causes these often-crippling anxieties? Since the fear of being a bag lady is, so far, not an authentic medical condition, the answers are speculative, but I spent a great deal of time and a lot of hard-earned money exploring the subject.

Some psychiatrists feel its origins are in abandonment, either by one's father or mother or both. The desertion doesn't have to be literal; most often it is an emotional distance or unavailability of a mother or, less commonly, a father.

As Dr. J pointed out, in my case, both my parents were distant. My mother's breakdown and her year in the hospital, which caused me to live with my grandmother, who was caring for her own dying daughter, contributed greatly to my sense of isolation and abandonment—both feelings that I imagine a real bag lady has to endure. There was no one I could rely on and thus I had to rely on myself. This was too much for a child of six to cope with. With no one to pay attention to my needs, as a child I feared that I would be dumped out into the world with no one and no resources to help me survive.

I mentioned before that when my mother came home from the hospital, I happened to be walking with her and holding her hand when I saw a real bag lady. I imagined that this frightening-looking old woman had been left alone, out in the freezing winds, with no home to go to, no one to help her. My fear of that bag lady was extremely powerful, but of course I couldn't articulate those feelings then. It was only with Dr. J that I began to see that I wasn't a child anymore, and as a functioning and successful adult I could certainly take care of myself.

Although I experienced a physically absent mother and a distant father, Dr. J explained that you can feel abandonment and insecurity from parents who divorce, who are self-oriented, or who are withholding, controlling, and emotionally absent.

Another origin of the syndrome is the lack of a cohesive sense of self. The feeling of a wholesome healthy self comes mostly from childhood nurturing, which bag lady syndrome sufferers may not have had. Those of us who haven't had this kind of unconditional loving background may feel a lack of self-worth, creating anxiety and depression in later years.

Tied to this lack of self-worth is a loss of or lack of an identity. *If I'm not worth much to anybody, who am I?* To put it in the plainest terms: A sense of self, an identity, means knowing who you are, what your strengths are, what your weaknesses are. If you don't think you have value, it's an easy step to imagine yourself on the streets with your tattered shopping bags. In actuality, as an adult you can have lots of money and success and a loving partner, but the irrational, childish fear is that you're really a worthless person whom society might just as well forget.

Over the three years that I saw Dr. J, the fears abated as he extracted the root causes, such as my mother's illness and the judgmental silent treatment that she indulged in when I had done something "wrong" as a child or "bad" as an adult, like writing a sex book.

I have always been grateful to both my parents for giving whatever love they were able to give, as they themselves had severely damaged childhoods. They gave me a college education and a comfortable life and instilled in me a love for learning, along with a love of fine things like silver and crystal. They believed absolutely in decency and honesty and charity and transmitted their solid values to me. I really didn't like them—or love them. And I felt enormous guilt about this. But wise Dr. J helped to rout that guilt.

"You don't have to like or to love your parents," he said. "What is necessary is to respect the institution of parenthood. If you honor and respect your parents simply because they were parents, you will avoid guilt, a powerful and crippling emotion that can cause serious dysfunction. The actions you take toward your parents—visits, calls, time spent together—are a recognition of your respect for the institution of parenthood; they do not need to be made from love."

....

As I continued to sit across from Dr. J every week, I felt myself growing stronger emotionally. On a practical level, I was more comfortable because I had a steady job and was saving every cent I could. Instead of feeling like the shattered glass I had described to him during one of our first sessions, at the end of our work together, I could portray myself as a filament of flexible steel, able to bend with the blows life might hammer me with, but not to break. Dr. J retired and I left *Self* and stable employment to return to freelancing and art. And slowly the bag lady nightmares began to intrude again.

I happened to be in Florida in 1999 on a magazine consulting job and decided to call Dr. J to say hello. It had been years since I'd seen him. He had long left his New York practice and was living in Florida. He was a serious golfer and world traveler but he continued to dispense his wisdom to his large group of friends, who constantly asked him for advice on problems. I knew of his doings because I'd kept up with him with a few phone calls each year, as I was so grateful to him. He was such an enormous part of my life that I still refer to him as "my father and my mother." In strict psychiatric protocol, I should have never become friendly with him, but he often said that he loved his patients and that love was the key to the cure, so he had several of us who stayed in touch with him.

Now he was a hearty and fit eighty-nine years old and still hitting the golf course with his wife every day. "Why don't you join me for lunch after my morning workout?" he suggested when I called. Over a tuna melt for him and a BLT for me at his golf club—I remember this meal most vividly—I mentioned that I was having bag lady dreams again.

"I'm not practicing anymore, as you know," he replied, "but you could spend years on a couch reanalyzing the issues we talked about long ago. You built a strong and enduring self and you've had many successes. My advice is, save every dollar you can and put it in a safe place. Knowing you have the security of your savings is the most pragmatic way to deal with your concerns."

We'd finished our sandwiches and were sipping iced coffee when he said, "I have a good idea for you. I have used the same investment man for thirty years. My daughters now have their money with him also. He makes a steady nine to eleven percent every year. He's completely dependable and trustworthy. Many of my friends have had their entire savings with him for decades. His fund is closed, but I think I know a way that I can get you in."

Thus, in what is my life's most exquisite irony, the man who had saved my life, psychologically speaking, now suggested I entrust my life's savings to a man named Bernard S. Madoff.

Do I bear Dr. J any ill will? Of course not! He was doing his best to help me. As he unfailingly did throughout the years that I was his patient. I still feel—and always will—

that he is the most influential person in my life. And, of course, I am still in touch with him.

So in 1999, on the recommendation of Dr. J, I was "allowed" to open an account with Bernard Madoff. I never met him. I spoke to him once for less than thirty seconds, when I'd finally demanded to at least hear the voice of the man who would be investing my hard-earned savings.

"Don't worry," he said, "your money will be safe with me." And that was the extent of our conversation.

CHAPTER 21

How to Look and Feel Good
When Recently Broke

I t is late February and I'm still in Florida, near the lavish lairs of the has-been billionaires, writing my book. I would prefer to be in my studio in New York working on my photographs, and mental claustrophobia is closing in as I try to write in a very small, very chilly kitchen. It's an overcast silvery-gray morning here, an unusually cool sixty-two degrees, and I'm staring at the computer waiting for words and sentences to materialize.

Usually if I reach a work impasse, I leave the studio and walk around, idly looking into windows and sometimes stepping into stores. That kind of no-destination wandering is a visually stimulating activity that clears my mind, allowing it to regenerate.

The other kind of shopping that I used to adore occurred

when Alex or Buffy or Sarah and I made a date for lunch and then played hooky from work for a few hours to check out the latest in Bergdorf or Barneys or to gaze—sometimes longingly—at the baubles at the jewelry market on Forty-seventh Street. I've always joked that shopping, whether you spend money or not, is female bonding at its highest, or lowest, level—and there's some truth to it.

Down here, I have no friends and no desire to do that fun kind of shopping. Desire and hope desert me at times. Just as words have abandoned me this morning.

Maybe driving will coax the words out of my brain. I'll take the old wagon out for a spin to clear my mind.

I'm cruising down Dixie Highway and feeling the need for a second jolt of coffee. I pull into a Guatemalan bakery–*cum*–coffee shop that is a favorite haunt of mine because the croissants are better than any I've ever had, including the ones at the Ritz in Paris. But an extra cup of java is not in my new budget. Nor will I ever see the Ritz again.

The hell with it, I say, and I am enjoying a double espresso and a warm-from-the-oven buttery croissant back in the driver's seat. Next to the bakery is a thrift shop, one I've visited in BMF times when I was on the lookout for glamorous bargains. Palm Beach thrift shops and consignment stores are famous for fab buys, because they are where rich ladies discard their couture clothes like used Diet Coke cans.

I finish my croissant and wonder whether I should peruse the offerings at Almost New All for You. The store benefits geriatric causes. I'll soon be geriatric myself so I should prepare to use their assistance.

Most likely because I can't face going back to the computer so soon, I walk into the shop, which is jammed with the worst furniture, the most badly painted canvases, the most tacky china and glassware imaginable—I'm certain it's all very costly stuff that tasteless owners cast off only to buy new gross and wasteful objects. But the treasure here is in the back: stacks of clothes that range from Gap workout gear to Valentino couture.

With the ingrained shopping habits of decades, I sort through the rusty old chrome racks. Nothing much of interest here today. The place is pretty well picked over. And on a scale of one to ten, my desire level is less than zero. I have not bought one thing since Madoff. As a Person of Reduced Circumstances, I feel that I will never buy anything again. However—

There *is* an item that catches my squinty editorial eye. A classically tailored Bill Blass gray sharkskin, pleated, silk-lined, hand-finished skirt that looks as if it will be a perfect fit. There are no dressing rooms in Almost New All for You, so I pull the skirt over my head, drop my jeans to my ankles, and find a small mirror where I can see about a third of myself. This piece of expensive cloth has my name on it.

Thirty bucks! Too much! Way too much! The white-haired volunteer at the cash register in her pink smock is a cement wall that will not budge on the price.

"It's designer," she tells me. "They don't go on sale."

"I'll have to think about it; that seems quite high," I tell her and walk back to my wagon. The original ticket was easily about a thousand bucks.

I owned many Blass suits when I had a clothing allowance. And Chanels, and Armanis, and Saint Laurents. They're still neatly packed in storage in my apartment basement. From time to time, I rummaged through the bunch and revived a special favorite by having the shoulder pads taken out or changing the hemlines according to the times. But those clothes, even if resurrected, are useless to me nowadays. It's a truism to say the world has changed: even President Obama sports khakis in the Oval Office. The fancy duds are headed for eBay or the closest consignment shop. In the past they would have been headed for a charity that helps down-and-out women who would have used the clothes for job interviews, but now they may make me a few dollars.

I leave the store but keep thinking about the elegant pleated Blass skirt. It's a classic. I wore similar ones in college with monogrammed Shetland sweaters and cashmere-blend kneesocks. I can wear this baby with flats or heels, with a cashmere sweater or a T-shirt. I have no clothing allowance, no clothing budget. I've got to figure out a way to look stylish and contemporary. If I look pulled together and tidy, I feel better.

I adored having a clothing allowance. Who wouldn't? It's the ultimate luxury. No, the ne plus ultra goody is a car and driver in New York City. I had them both!

But I was very careful in the way I spent my allowance dollars. I nailed several Hermès bags; a few watches; a Buccellati ring; earrings; and my favorite piece of jewelry, a strand of luscious baroque pearls that I still wear almost every day. Most of my office and evening outfits were from designers who were delighted to sell editors items at cost or give them away free so that we would be seen in them at the Four Seasons, movie premieres, trendy new eateries, or other paparazzi-laden haunts.

I limited my purchases strictly to best-quality name-brand stuff like Franck Muller or Cartier watches because, very consciously, I thought, if I ever needed the money, these baubles might be worth something. And I may have been right.

Still, a question plagued me during these years. Was I superficial, did I care too much about how I dressed, how my apartment looked? As I accumulated some of the beautiful things I had always admired, I suffered guilt and embarrassment that I was the empress of shallowness, that necessary and useful clothes and a Timex watch were all that a "serious person" needed.

Now I like to say I'm "deeply superficial," and what I mean by that is that I put a lot of effort into having my surroundings and the way I look and the work I do measure up to my aesthetic and intellectual ideals. I don't care about this year's trends. Well, I must admit sometimes I can be seduced by something that's new or something I've never seen before, but what is most important is honesty, authenticity, integrity, and a dash of style in my physical surroundings. If an object or item of clothing is, in addition, truly original—a rare occurrence—I value it even more.

A white shirt that's designed to fit the body well and

comfortably and is made of good, lasting cloth with well-sewn buttons and no unnecessary frills is something that I prize and respect. I'd like to be able to collect art that meets all the criteria I've set out above, but most often the work I would like to own is way beyond my means. I try like hell to make my own work fit those standards. One never reaches "the ideal," but the attempts have kept me going for so many years.

....

I turn the wagon around and march back to the thrift shop. I carefully count out the thirty dollars for it because it is a classic. My new PoRC style is *all* about "classic." Clothes, jewelry, and accessories that endure.

Classics, for PoRCs or WoCAs (Women of a Certain Age) like me are the best style bet because they last and never turn you into a fashion victim. Classic dressing saves me time, decisions, trips to stores to return items, and wastes none of the money I hope to earn. I have a look and I feel good in it.

Nice clothes aren't the only luxury to which I've grown accustomed. Over the years—starting with my beauty editor job at *Glamour*—I've morphed into a spoiled beauty princess. How will I ever afford haircuts, hair color, dermatology? None of these comes cheap. But if you're poor, you become wily and resourceful. It's one of the benefits of a very restricted budget.

I have a new idea—actually it's an old idea that I plan to dust off and put to use. Artists have always relied on swapping goods for services. A painter friend of mine recently exchanged a large abstract work for a gorgeous emerald engagement ring for his lady love. Lawyers and doctors have become major collectors by trading their services for works of art.

Each of us has something of worth to barter. It could be the silver spoon that graced your mouth at birth, an antique purse, closet organizing—anything that might have value that another might be willing to consider as swappable for something else. In extreme cases of need, PoRCs have even been known to barter their bodies, but this is certainly not in the stars for me.

My present state has made me much less bashful about asking for things than I was in pre-MF days. I've never been a person who asks for discounts, for special treatment, for freebies. I finally screwed up my courage a few weeks ago and asked if I could trade a photographic portrait for a beauty treatment. It worked! So, as soon as I find myself looking a bit more tattered, worn, and wrinkled, I'm offering photographs or even slightly rusty editing skills in exchange for blond highlights, a mini face-lift, veneering of chipped teeth, collagen, Botox. Swapping would never have occurred to me unless my entire life had changed. When your worst nightmare comes true, you discover valuable things about your self and your world. I certainly don't wish my semester in hell on anyone, but I do want to recommend thinking of adversity in a more positive way.

One of my unexpected experiences recently was a talk I gave to a group in California. I'd had dinner the night before with two of the women who organized the lunch, and they asked me about my speech. I'd planned to say how I got involved with the MF, reveal some dishy magazine experiences, and provide a minute or two of the background of the pink ribbon, which they'd specifically asked for. Over a dessert coffee they asked me what knowledge I'd gained from my experiences and I told them I'd surely learned plenty.

Back in my room, I decided to dump the original talk I had outlined for the lunch and, based on our conversation, I pounded out the following list of what knowledge I'd gained over the past few months, much of which made it into this book.

> If your worst fears happen, you live through them. They can be as bad as you imagined them but somehow you manage.
> You will surprise yourself at how well you cope. You have enormous resources you don't know about.
> You are in control until you have no mind left.
> When you're flooded with anxiety or panic, *think*—don't feel.
> There is such a word as "no." Use it to protect yourself.
> Indulge your crazy ideas—just think a bit about the consequences first.
> You don't have to love your parents. Honor and respect the institution of parenthood, and you will feel no guilt.
> There is no such thing as human worthlessness. Even the MF must have

some redeeming quality, although I admit I
doubt it.

People will always surprise you, with their
generosity or their nastiness.

You're sunk if you lose your sense of humor.

Ask for what you want even if you think you
won't get It. You'll be surprised at the
response sixty percent of the time.

It's okay to feel pity for yourself—for a short
while.

Ranting out loud can make you feel quite a bit
better.

Stop negative thinking any way you can. It
takes discipline but you can do it.

Fear has two faces: the good side motivates
you, the bad side paralyzes you.

When you have your first sip of coffee in the
morning, stop for a full ten seconds and
taste how good it is.

Decide on a short-term goal and a long-term
goal and give them your very best shot.

Don't beat yourself up about a decision: it was
right at the time you made it.

If you can't make a decision, you can always
decide not to decide.

You have a self. Know its strengths and
weaknesses.

Fear can make you tougher and stronger.

Evil exists.

Generosity can trump almost anything.

Expect the unexpected, but there is no way to
prepare for it.

Change is inevitable but it's an adventure.

Loss happens. Get used to it.

Be a fighter; life's no fun if you're not.

CHAPTER 22

The Bag Lady Throws a Party

One of my close friends, Eleanor, who, with her husband, has an adorable cottage here in Florida, is having a birthday and my present to her will be a small party in the friend's house where I'm staying. Could it have been only five months ago that I was getting ready to entertain some pals in New York, putting the finishing touches on my elegant tulip-and-freesia-adorned pear-wood dinner table in New York, when I heard the news about the MF? I thought I'd never give a party again.

This get-together will be quite a bit different in style. Eight is the most this little place—and I—can handle, as there is no dining room, scant and unmatched cutlery, odds and ends of china, and only a few glasses.

My BMF party routine would have involved planning ahead for days with too much stupid fretting and worrying about

> guest list
>
> invitations
>
> hors d'oeuvres, first course, second course,
>> possibly a third course, dessert(s)
>
> flowers
>
> wines, liquors, liqueurs,
>> nonalcoholic beverages
>
> seating plans
>
> pretty table settings: lustrous silver, spotless
>> china, gleaming crystal, immaculate
>> napkins, perfectly ironed place mats
>
> appropriately dressy white shirt
>
> candle and ice supply
>
> caterers, freelance chefs, and bartender
>
> helpers to man and clean up the kitchen

Looking at this long, pretentious list, I realize I must have been a lunatic or a masochist to live like that! My brand-new party ethic is time-efficient, financially sound, and stress-free. I now intend to adhere strictly to these rules:

> no fuss,
>
> no muss,
>
> and almost no money.

But can I pull this off with people who frequent soirees where pre-meltdown Iranian caviar and crystal-fluted Dom P are served without pause by an attentive and attractive staff?

....

I head to Publix, the nearest supermarket. Although I try to be a good citizen of the earth and I am aware that using paper kills trees and plastic pollutes the planet, I choose for one night not to think about the consequences of my purchases. On all the kitchen counters, I lay out long sheets of cheap white shelving paper. I stack bright yellow, red, green, blue, and purple paper plates; matching napkins; and red and yellow plastic forks and knives on the white paper. I heap on a few dozen colored plastic cups for wine, water, and Diet Coke. I fill ten or twelve of the cups with giant hibiscus flowers and dark, glossy tropical leaves from the backyard and scatter them on the counters, the coffee table, and in the bathroom. Luckily the owner of the house likes votive candles, so I distribute a half dozen in the small living room, which will just about accommodate the group if a couple of us sit on the floor. All this preparation takes not days or hours, but about fifteen minutes. I'm not counting the quick trip to Publix because it was more fun than work.

The eight guests are greeted with my one splurge—iced Grey Goose martinis served in glasses from the cupboard's mélange of glassware. I give the sole holdout an inexpensive white Italian wine the liquor store man recommended that turns out to be quite good. The hors d'oeuvres consist of the olives in the drinks and a small plate of them on the coffee table.

I must admit I concoct a mean martini and the party is warming up when the doorbell rings and six pizzas are delivered. I phoned earlier to order five but the pizza man offered to give me an extra one because they were for a birthday celebration. I can say with certainty that all of us women, and probably some of the men, are watching our carbs and our calories but at the end not one slice remains. I bought two bottles of the wine, hoping we'd finish only one, but both vanished. Needless to say, the Grey Goose disappeared earlier in the evening.

Birthday cakes are expensive. To save the most money I would have baked one myself but that meant purchasing pans and ingredients I wouldn't use again, so I decided to buy the most superlative birthday cake I could think of.

Carvel's Fudgie the Whale cake ain't a rock-bottom bargain but it's an all-time favorite of mine and, again, I reckoned that, after so many carb-freighted pizzas, I'd cut small pieces and the guests would politely take a couple of bites and I'd have a week of leftover chocolate nirvana. Dear, divine Fudgie is gobbled up in no time and I find one of the guests in the kitchen unabashedly licking the last of the chocolate crumbs off her fingers.

It was a no-stress, great-fun night. I even had a good time! Usually I'm wiped out after throwing a dinner party, but aside from washing the martini glasses and the cake knife and loading the dishwasher with the sturdy plastic utensils that I would keep again for the next time, the cleanup consisted of a short walk to the garbage container.

PoRC entertaining is easy and fun. I can't afford it often but when I return to New York, I'm going to research the best and cheapest neighborhood pizza place I can find. (My memories of the Domino's Christmastime rip-off are still fresh.) I'll lay in a good supply of reusable plastic glasses, knives, and forks and a major stack of recycled colored paper plates. I'll even cut out place mats from plain brown wrapping paper and fill some of the plastic cups with fat Crayolas the way I did when my son and I lived on West Broadway. I probably still have some of those drawings and funny, crazy jottings that my friends and I did after we'd downed a few glasses of Chianti.

My little house in Florida has just sold for about forty percent less than I put into it but I'm glad I don't have the responsibility for it anymore. The small amount of cash I received will help with daily living expenses and, if I can earn some more money, it may be the basis of a careful, new savings plan.

I'm back in the city now. Paul and I are together much of the time when he's not in his studio. He's a painter and work isn't selling, but we're having fun. I haven't yet figured out a way to afford a cheap studio of my own or to share one, but if I can't think of something, I'll work in my living room the way I used to. I'm planning to start a portrait business in the fall. I'm still waiting to see if I can retrieve the SIPC insurance owed to me, but I'm glad to report that it's looking good from what I read and hear. The Long Island house is still for sale. In other news, this week the MF has been sentenced to 150 years in prison. I hope he lives a very long life.

I think back to the question: Is it worse to have money and lose it or never to have it at all? The thing about *not* ever having money is that you always think it will make your life better and you will be happier. But you are not aware of its flaws. Once you've had money, you will probably miss the luxuries and experiences it can buy, but at least you're aware that it's not all it's cracked up to be.

No one gave me a dollar or a valuable contact to start out with and it's been satisfying to earn money all on my own. The glitzy and gritty jobs I had in the course of working for that money allowed me to have an adventurous and interesting life, to meet a wide spectrum of people, to travel to exotic places, to own a house and an apartment and beautiful things. I didn't squander what I earned, I saved it, and, for the most part, I believe I spent it wisely. When I knew it was gone, I had to start all over again. I was enraged, of course, but it was an impotent anger. Instead of endlessly picturing vile things that should happen to the MF, what I really want to see is what kind of new life I can create. Maybe my unremitting curiosity is what keeps me going.

What would have happened if the economy had maintained its upward swing indefinitely? Many smart people believed that would be the case. I would have continued to take out enough of my retirement savings each year to live on—not an extravagant life, but a comfortable one. I would have kept the studio, made art, tried to sell it, faced the ups and downs of health and family issues, and generally remained on the same path.

With the catastrophic upheaval of my finances I must think and act in new ways. As I've said, it's the uncertainty of everything in my life that unhinges me. But that uncertainty is a fact, and I must accept it.

It's been a stunning six months in every way, but I'm fully here and alive as never before. I've written this book and I'm spending more time with my son and my niece and their families. I've worked on a photographic series of the dolls titled *After Madoff*. I posed the girls as they deflated in car accidents, drowned in luxe swimming pools, were hanged by their Gucci silk scarves, and collapsed into their own fake Birkin bags—all scenarios tied to their recent destruction and, by proxy, mine, through the evil machinations of the MF. I'm having a show of them in New York in the fall.

I'm enjoying Paul and my friends, feasting on pizza, counting my calories as always, and nipping negative thoughts as best I can. Every morning I take a new and exhilarating pleasure in my first sip of steaming coffee as I look out my window at a changed and beautiful and fascinating world. I do not exaggerate when I say I can't wait to take my shower, button on a snappy white self-ironed Lands' End shirt and well-worn Levis, and get out and about to see what will happen next.

So—was it better to have it and then lose it? Yes, yes, yes! Even though I lived with horrible bag lady fears of losing it all, now that those financial fears have materialized, I'm in pretty good shape and looking to what's next. Experiences— good and bad, exciting and boring, tragic and absurd— make up a life. Not to have lived to the fullest is the saddest, most irresponsible life I can think of.

ACKNOWLEDGMENTS

I continue to be astonished at the generosity of friends and colleagues who have responded to my AMF situation. Where would I be without Ed Victor, my very dear friend, the superagent, who sold this book and has been in touch with me practically every day since December 11. And ditto Ellen Archer, Hyperion's fast-acting publisher, who immediately tuned in to the bag lady fears that so many women face and contributed many important editorial ideas to this book.

It was not a piece of cake to write about my MF experience and it felt as if I were reliving those horrible days as I went over the manuscript. Barbara Jones was a gentle and determined editor who helped in every way. Gillian Blake, an editorial mastermind, was a key force in shaping the book, and her additions and suggestions have been invaluable. Tina Brown of TheDailyBeast.com instantly gave me a blogging podium to vent from, and Jane Spencer helped to structure my rants.

What would I do without Richard Story and Alex Mayes Birnbaum and Patty Matson? They literally took me by the hand and helped me back to sanity with their love, kindness, and pragmatism.

I absolutely could not have survived without Bob Littman.

Tommy and Alice—and Maude, Joseph, Abigail, and our Louise—there's no way to thank you adequately for your small and large kindnesses! Patty Marx gave me many serious ideas for this book while making me laugh so much that I almost choked to death on a Diet Coke. Paul Wilmot knows how to make the sun shine, and while doing that serves up the best stone crabs and champagne on the East Coast. Buffy Easton's insights, sharp eye, and smart advice will always be heeded. And Sarah Rosenthal is a friend who can restore emotional balance with a telephone call.

The thoughtfulness of friends, colleagues, and strangers was something I could never have imagined. I could write paragraphs on each one, but I know if you got this far, you most probably want me to wrap it up. So, in alphabetical order, here you are . . . I've probably left out out more than I've included, but you all know who you are and I hope you know how grateful I am to you.

Chris Albrecht; Annette and Joe Allen; Joanne Casullo, one of the most generous women I've ever met; Cathryn Collins; Amy Fine Collins; Sheila Donnelly and Paul Theroux; Jamie Drake; Michael Fuchs, my extraordinary friend and dealer; major life-savers Barbara and Eric Hippeau; most amazing Jane, Michael, and Katie Hoffman; Gerry Imber; Jae Man Joo; Munnu Kasliwal all the way from Jaipur; Anne Keating; compassionate Eleanore and Michael Kennedy; Judy Kent; Phil Kent, stealth adviser; Andrew Kirk; Julie Lavin; Suzanne Lengyel, my banker through worse and better; Evvie

Lipper and Bill Speck; Imke Littman; Harry Lodge, physician and soul-doctor; Michael and Alice Martell, lifelong life advisers; Tom and Lucille Mathews; ever-there Evan McGlinn; super strategist Sandi Mendelson; my stalwart Stuart Miller; Burtie Minkoff of the eagle eye and the huge heart; Patty Newburger and Brad Wechsler; sister pal Nancy Novogrod; Priscilla Ratazzi, a true friend in deed; angelo Steve Rubin; fellow-traveler Deborah Sharpe; Sharon Stein; Susan Steinthal, a brilliant legal tactician; Bettina Sulser; J. D. Talasek; Stefano Tonchi; Stellene Vollandes; the ever-generous Nick von Hoffman (and Schnitzel); Leslie Westreich; Anna Wintour; and Penelope Weld of the unforgettable letter.

Because too much type gives eye-glaze, here's another part of the same list: Will Ameringer; Carole Baron; Marie Brenner; Holly Brubach; Larry Burstein; Amy Cappellazzo; Susan Carey; Richard Cohen; David Patrick Columbia; Faye Cone; Jennifer Crandall and Zach Story; Suzanne Donaldson; Lisa Gabor; Sarah Gavlak; Adam Gopnik and Martha Parker; Betsy Gotbaum; David and Melanie Holland; Stephen Jacoby; Joel Kassimir; Peter Kaufman, early responder and major connector; Frank and Bobbi Kitchens; Wayne Koestenbaum; Leslie Krause; Iris Marden and the Fedorkos; David Maupin; David Meitus and Angela Westwater; Kathryn Mondadori; Si and Victoria Newhouse; Richard Pandiscio; Jana Pasquel; Christine Romans; Paul Roossin; Donna Rosen; Bernard Scharf; Paul Scherer; Michael and Lisa Schultz, and Maggie and Lucy; Nicholas Sopkin; James Spodnik; Elizabeth Sussman; Andrew and Ann Tisch; Billie Tisch; Laurie Tisch; Elisabeth Tretter; James Truman for fine words and wine;

Alfred Vachris and Thomas Molesky, tech gods as well as friends; Emily Vaughan; Carol Ryan Victor; Alex von Bidder; Diane von Furstenburg; Jim and Rita Wetzler; Kyle White, Tommy Buckett, and Hiroshi, who tend the locks; Yolanda; Zezé, Peggy, Doris, and Walter; and Jake Zemansky. And the California contingent—Bob Bookman; Mary Elizabeth and Nancy Eileen, who are friends of Leon's; and Bruce Vinocur and Jo Ann Chase, aka "Ruthie."

And to my small and precious family, for providing the solid ground on which I was able to rebuild my equilibrium and regain my sense of humor: John and Julie Rousseau Penney and most enchanting Celeste (who finally found the elusive Tuna B Fish), and Erin and Paul Scott and adorable Otis and Lilah (who unfailingly beats me at Russian bank). And thanks from my soul to Dennis Ashbaugh—steadfast and true.